THE
ROMANTIC GARDEN

THE
ROMANTIC
GARDEN

GRAHAM ROSE

**Illustrations by
PAUL COX**

VIKING

VIKING
Viking Penguin Inc., 40 West 23rd Street, New York, New York 10010, U.S.A.
Penguin Books Canada Limited, 2801 John Street, Markham, Ontario, Canada L3R 1B4

First published in 1988 by Viking Penguin Inc. in simultaneous hardcover
and paperback editions

Published simultaneously in Great Britain by Frances Lincoln Limited

The Romantic Garden was conceived, edited, and designed by Frances Lincoln
Limited, Apollo Works, 5 Charlton Kings Road, London NW5 2SB.

ISBN 0-670-82068-7
Library of Congress Catalog Card Number 87-40316
(CIP data available)

Printed in Hong Kong
by Kwong Fat
Typeset in Bembo by
Bookworm Typesetting Manchester

CONTENTS

FOREWORD

If you ask many people to lean back in a comfortable chair, close their eyes and imagine their ideal garden, I believe that it is likely that their visions will have a lot in common. Essentially this Eden will be a very leafy place, with a tracery of delicate twigs and foliage seen in silhouette against the sky or framing every vista, in contrast to a brighter area beyond. Bolder forms, too, will be present to command attention and provide interest and variety. While it will be flower-filled and colorful, the tones will tend to be pastel and subtly integrated, with only here and there a more vivid area contrived with the greatest restraint to attract the eye.

The mood induced by the garden will be one of a charmed and highly fragrant calm as an antidote to the nervous jostle of everyday life. Although much of the garden will be imbued with a comforting sense of seclusion, with attractive screens enclosing secret areas, it will also liberate the spirit by offering glimpses of enchanting views.

There may be hints of former, nobler times. The tracks of overgrown pathways and portions of ruined buildings and relics of ornaments or idols might be encountered during the garden journey. Their masonry would serve as a wonderful foil for flowers and foliage, and they would also make fine alcoves or backgrounds for seats placed to provoke contemplation.

Since no-one's elysium could be complete unless it contained the life-sustaining element of water, it will be present in the form of gurgling streams or splashing fountains, or mirroring the changing sky and surrounding vegetation in the still surface of basins and ponds, or introducing a shiver of excitement in the shadowy moist dankness of fern-flanked grottos.

In short, I believe that most people would like their homes to be surrounded by an extremely romantic place. This book is an attempt to show them how it can be made. Many people have helped me in this endeavor. My special thanks are due to Paul Cox for his splendid visual interpretations of features described in the text, and to Sarah Mitchell, Louise Tucker and Caroline Hillier of Frances Lincoln Ltd for their excellent work in editing and laying out the book. I would like to thank Susan Berry for suggesting the idea.

I am also grateful to Robin Williams for his clear display of the plans of the fine romantic gardens whose owners and designers – including Arabella Lennox-Boyd, John and Roger Last, John Codrington, Mr and Mrs Levitan, Mr R J Dykes and Mr and Mrs Canneman-Philipse – kindly allowed them to be featured.

Helpful suggestions and advice in the preparation of the book were received from many friends, with Richard and Imogen Carter Jonas, Elisabeth Goldbach, Peter King, Rosemary Verey, France Phillips, Alain and Aline de la Prunarede, Elizabeth McLean, Dorothy Sheffield and my wife notable among them. Finally, grateful thanks are due to Jeanette Lazell for all her help on the manuscript.

Graham Rose

INTRODUCING THE ROMANTIC GARDEN

The adjective 'romantic' is often used to describe works of art of a particular kind, including gardens of the type discussed in this book. Appropriately, it stems from the word 'romance' – originally a medieval tale of chivalry, with scenes and incidents remote from ordinary life. There's a further happy connection too, in that a romancer – the word derives from the same root – can be defined as 'one who deals in extravagant fictions; a fantastic liar'. For that is, in a happy sense, what many great garden designers are: truly talented people who contrive to make us ignore the world outside and believe that the impossible is readily attainable. The very best among them can take a miserable yard and, by clever construction and planting, lead us down an enchanting track to an idyllic corner of Arcadia, while blinding us to eyesores beyond and suppressing our awareness of noisy neighbors or the rumbling trucks that throng the road outside its walls.

It is this ability to exclude reason and appeal directly to the senses that produces the loudest gasps of admiration from visitors to fine gardens, no matter what their scale or predominant style. Even in many of the greatest formal gardens, there are often small romantic areas along their margins, where the mathematical precision of the overall plan has been ignored or neglected, which offer infinite delight. They are the corners where plants seem to have been placed haphazardly and allowed to rampage and flower without constriction. Of course their innocent allure often conceals much true gardening art. But it is

certainly a style of garden that most of us would be happiest to live with, and it is a style that we can readily learn to create ourselves.

THE ROMANTIC LANDSCAPE

It may seem strange that romantic designs, which have remained popular since they were evolved three centuries ago, should have been created so late in the nearly six thousand years during which people have been designing gardens for pleasure. But for most of that time, artists, including garden designers, were patronized by powerful princes of state and church who demanded works that confirmed their dominance over, or impressed their beliefs upon, humbler folk. In architecture and landscaping, rigid formality of style best served this purpose. Painters were favored who adopted a set formula for producing pictures, in which all the characters were clearly identifiable – not only by their appearance, but also by their gestures and place on the canvas. Eventually, however, various factors, including a developing merchant class of more diverse taste who could provide the arts with much wider patronage, freed artists from such constrictions.

Three great painters working in Rome and Naples in the seventeenth century reflected the way in which many of their fellow arists were thinking. Claude Lorraine, Gaspard Poussin (Gaspard Dughet) and Salvator Rosa all continued to represent the established themes – the

This closely planted avenue of beeches, culminating in a statue of a phoenix, epitomizes romantic gardening in the grand manner. The atmosphere created is spiritual and other-worldly. The soaring trunks of the trees and their overhead canopy make a tunnel of mysterious subdued green light in contrast to the brightness in the glade beyond. Romantic garden designers can also create these effects of light and shade on a smaller and more intimate scale.

biblical stories and the myths and allegories of antiquity. But, for them, the setting became more important than the story. The main theme was often reduced to a group of figures occupying a small area, on a vast canvas displaying a wide landscape. It is in those landscapes that we can discover the germ of a movement that has led to some of the best in many arts, including the making of gardens.

For while, at first glance, the landscapes appear 'natural' they were, in fact, highly romanticized – truly fantastic lies. Although features on the canvas can be identified in the topography of the countryside round Rome or Naples in which the painters roamed, none of them can actually be seen from a single viewpoint. The painters selected the best features and reassembled them into wonderful romantic compositions – altering the gradient of the slope here, changing the profile of a hill there or crowning it with a ruined temple if an eye-catching feature was demanded by the composition. And ordinary people, farmers, shepherds, woodmen and swineherds were portrayed going about their ordinary business in a charming and idealized way.

The English art historian Sir Kenneth Clark described paintings by these artists as 'representations of the most enchanting dream which

RIGHT A raging torrent, storm-blasted trees, crumbling masonry and daunting crags dominate this fine Landscape with a Bridge *by Salvator Rosa. The romance of the landscape captures the imagination, and the horsemen and pedestrians play a barely significant role. It is a far cry from the formality of early Renaissance painting, and represents one of the earliest examples of the romantic movement which inspired landscape gardeners like William Kent to think about garden design in a new way.*

BELOW Marie Antoinette's Hameau *at Versailles was a romantic idyll – an idealized version of rural life to which she could retreat when bored with the formality of the court. The careful attention to detail, shown in the buildings and the miniature landscape of the* Petit Trianon *surrounding it, demonstrates the strength of the appeal of the romantic movement in the 18th century.*

has ever consoled mankind, the myth of a golden age in which man lived on the fruits of the earth, peacefully, piously and with primitive simplicity – an earthly paradise . . . a harmony between man and nature'.

This was certainly a vision cherished by the young English painter and landscape architect William Kent, a great admirer of Claude, Poussin and Rosa. At Rousham, near Oxford, between 1720 and 1725, Kent was given free reign to design a garden entirely to his own taste which can still be seen today. One section, called the Venus glade, is thickly shaded by yew trees and contains an icy plunge drained by a meandering rill. It is quintessentially romantic and represents one of the best early examples of gardening in this style.

Even on a sunny day, the light among the fringing yews is a subdued, cooling green. The canopy is thinner close to the stream and, when the sun is directly overhead, it strikes through in distinct bright shafts to dapple the ground, spotlighting and bringing into high relief gently arched fronds of fern. Attracted by the sparkle and gurgle of water in the rill, dragonflies caught in a beam seem momentarily mesmerized and flash a brilliant kaleidoscope of colors as their wings vibrate. Hovering, they resemble the blooms of stemless, exotic plants, whose presence seems natural when breathing the slightly inebriating, resinous air. The whole atmosphere in the glade is so other-worldly that entering it after strolling over the hot, bright blandness of an open lawn provokes a frisson of excitement. This was the type of assault on all the perceptions that Kent and all subsequent romantic gardeners aimed to contrive, and which no formal Renaissance garden, with its areas of terrace and battery of sculpture, could provide.

It wasn't long before Kent's obvious revulsion from the dry classicism of previous epochs was shared by artists of many types. Even the lofty, whose lifestyles followed a rigid curriculum in surroundings of classical grandeur, were obviously tempted by visions of a freer existence. After she married the future Louis XVI, Marie-Antoinette soon sickened of the tedium of courtly life at Versailles. So she had a highly romantic model farm and water mill built in the grounds of the Petit Trianon pavilion, which still charms visitors to Versailles. There she and her fellow courtiers could play at living the idyllic simple life. Of course it was all another 'extravagant fiction'. Although the cows they milked were real, the life encompassed none of the brutishness and hardship suffered by the peasantry. If cows misbehaved and soiled the courtiers' boots, the boots were simply discarded and passed to servants for cleaning.

THE APPEAL
—OF THE ROMANTIC—
GARDEN

LEFT This wonderful
jumble of plants spilling
over the pathway between
the beds, showing little
evidence of restraint, is a
fine example of good
romantic planting.

BELOW Lush planting and
careful choice of pretty
materials and artefacts –
especially the decorative
trelliswork thickly overhung
with climbers – has turned
this tiny roof garden into a
secret and romantic haven.

The romantic movement, in art and landscape, received its greatest impetus at a time when the horrors of the industrial revolution were being recognized; when most people's lives were becoming dominated by relentlessly demanding machines and were passed in noisy, crowded and insanitary cities. It was a period when anything distracting, which appealed purely to the spirit, was naturally welcomed. But while conditions may have changed substantially today, modern life in what we call 'post-industrial' society does involve carrying a heavy burden of jostle and tension. And the romantic approach certainly offers a wonderfully soothing way of escaping from the harassment of everyday life in our leisure hours.

No matter how many novel attitudes toward garden design have arisen since the emergence of the romantic landscape, romantic gardens have continued to have a strong appeal to home owners everywhere. Their evergreen popularity is probably due to their continuing role as a distraction from the cares of everyday life. And, as the pace of living increases, the popularity of romantic gardens is likely to grow.

CREATING THE ROMANCE

The aim of this book is to inspire and tell gardeners how to make gardens that appeal to all the senses; fragrant, visually unusual and beautiful places that mute extraneous sound and which soothe the spirits; gardens that appeal to emotion rather than to reason.

To be successful, romantic gardens must meet certain criteria, whatever their size or the particular elements which they contain. Above all they must be places isolated from the everyday world, where there are no reminders of the normal working day. To ensure this feeling of isolation the planning must be very thorough. Paving, when used in the garden, mustn't bear any resemblance to paving in the streets. In cities, the garden boundaries must obscure the presence of any other buildings in the district. In the country, idealized views over attractive landscapes with glimpses of such features as church spires or unpolluted streams, or thick woodland can be admitted.

Inside the boundaries, it should never be possible to see all other areas of a romantic garden from any one viewpoint. Even in small gardens there should be hidden corners from which it is impossible to see the house. By thoughtful planting and placement of screens and other artefacts, achieving this sense of seclusion

is not as difficult as it seems. And when you have obtained it, the garden will have acquired such a desirable, mysterious quality that a visitor wouldn't be too surprised to encounter a sinuous heraldic leopard wandering benignly through its thick foliage. Good romantic gardens should be capable of invoking flights of fantasy as a therapeutic distraction from such mundane worries as work and how the bills are ever going to be paid.

The profusion and lax abundance of plant life in a garden of this type should also be a refreshing display of the bounty of nature. It will remind you that there are other worlds and lifestyles than those rigid concrete jungles with their compelling timetables which many of us are obliged to inhabit. And, after quelling our everyday frustrations, romantic gardens ought also to foster nobler contemplation – or even sometimes a cathartic melancholy. In some areas, the juxtaposition of ancient-looking masonry or statuary and rampant plants might introduce a poignant echo of an idealized past. Nevertheless, since when making a romantic garden the aim is to create a world of fantasy, there is no reason why it should be also deprived of a sense of fun. The garden can contain amusing and surprising *trompe l'oeil* – cunning optical illusions – or just charming figures stumbled upon by accident, which have the capacity to shock or raise a smile.

GARDENS OF _INSPIRATION_

Opportunities to sample the flavor of the romantic in gardening exist almost everywhere. Most notably, they can be encountered at the conjunction between the densely and more sparsely planted areas of many of the world's great woodland gardens, particularly where such areas contain an informal water feature. But I have also been struck by the romantic appeal of some of the less intensely cultivated areas in gardens famous for more formal characteristics. It is certainly present in the wilder lower section of the charming, small, Bartram garden in Philadelphia or round the lake area of the Arnold Arboretum in the same city. The smoke-charred ruins that prop up the giant wisteria at Nymans in Sussex would provide a satisfactory backdrop for any Gothic fantasy, as would the azalea-lined steps that scale the side of the Glen at Glenveagh in Ireland.

Happily, romantic effects can be obtained just as readily in tiny gardens as they can in vast parks. I have seen yards of less than 20 sq m/200 sq ft located in central areas of throbbing cities like London, Paris and New York, which seemed to embody as much feeling of mystery and delight as the canvases of the best romantic painters.

To people born in northern temperate areas of the world, it is natural to associate the romantic tradition with gardens in which deep shade, dark evergreen foliage and ancient ivy-clad trees predominate. But it has no such constricting geographic or climatic limitations, and it is possible to make romantic gardens in the tropics or areas with a hot, dry climate. There are wonderfully romantic areas in the grounds of the Huntingdon Collection near Los Angeles, in which the outside world seems utterly banished. And strolling beneath the rose-heavy pergolas that shade the paths at La Mortola, near Ventimiglia on the Italian Riviera, it is impossible to imagine that the whirring roulette wheels of the Monte Carlo Casino are less than a half-hour's drive away from that patch of Elysium.

Many might consider the garden at Le Colombier, near Villadonnel in the Midi of France, to have 'gone to seed'. But to anyone privileged to see it and with only a modicum of sensitivity, it is a paradise. Having long escaped from the confines of their corroding iron obelisks, classical climbing and rambling roses struggle to amaze with the profusion of their intertwining stems and highly scented, cabbagey blooms. Elsewhere, weeping sophora trees hang their tresses of white-petaled flowers in the shade of umbrella

RIGHT This gloriously romantic flight of steps at La Mortola in Italy shows how well such features look if they and their surroundings are not too well groomed. There is something very attractive about plants which have established themselves in the gaps between stone paving and been allowed to grow unchecked.

pines. In the autumn it seems criminal to walk among them, for fear of crushing the hundreds of thousands of exquisite, tiny *Cyclamen neapolitanum*. These spread in great rose pink swathes at the feet of the trees, on ground which once carried closely mown lawn which has reverted to a magic meadow.

In fact, very often the most romantic effects have been achieved by accident, when time and nature have wreaked their own designs on what were previously rather formal layouts. At Dromoland Castle, in Ireland, there is excitement in discovering relics of pools, with carved stone surroundings, among seedling sycamores, which have sprouted like nettles. Outlying areas of the parks surrounding the Chateaux of the Loire often offer similar delightful surprises. And surprise, too, is appropriate, because, as Oscar Wilde pointed out 'The very essence of romance is uncertainty'.

CREATING THE SANCTUARY

erhaps the most vital aspect of any romantic garden is that it should provide you with a strong feeling of sanctuary. It should offer an escape from reality, a tranquil haven with an atmosphere of mystery and antiquity set within the beauties that nature offers the senses. So that you may be transported away from everyday cares into this inviting and secret world, your first consideration in creating your own romantic garden must be to ensure seclusion. The garden must be 'a fine and private place', fully enclosed and guarding its secrets from the uninvited.

EXCLUDING THE OUTSIDE WORLD

If the world outside is to be banished, then the outer framework of the garden must provide as effective a screen as possible. This will cut out the world beyond and preserve the inner sense of sanctuary by hindering observation from outside and making the world inside totally compelling. The most romantic gardens are undoubtedly those enclosed by old high walls, and the lucky few may have the opportunity to take over a garden that offers immediately the sense of changeless calm and security that only mellow brick or stone walls can give. Most, however, may well be faced with the problem of creating this same feeling on a more modern and more open plot, where it will be quite a challenge to exclude the outside world.

WALLS

By far the most satisfactory way of isolating a garden is to surround it with a stone or brick wall. It provides an effective and impenetrable screen, muffling noise and giving all the shelter and privacy essential to the creation of the romantic garden. As long as you are aware of the possible wind-tunnel effects of high walls, the possible alkalinity of the soil beneath them and the almost certain dryness, you can take advantage of their benefits. Walls of a suitable aspect can be used to shelter the more tender and spectacular plants that add so much to the lush and rather overgrown air of the perfect romantic garden. You may well have a chance to grow plants usually associated with the rich gardens of the deep south. *Magnolia grandiflora* 'Edith Bogue' and *Camellia japonica* provide deep evergreen glossy foliage and voluptuous flowers over a long season. In very cold gardens, *Magnolia virginiana* will give a similar effect.

The best possible wall for a garden is one of soft-colored stone in irregularly shaped pieces, festooned with trailing plants. It will always look attractive, and its old-worldliness, in itself, bestows a romantic feeling upon the area it encloses. There is no doubt that finding capable craftsmen and good raw materials can be difficult in some areas and inevitably, if available, they will be expensive. But certainly anyone who has such a wall built seems to think it was worth depriving themselves of other luxuries to be able to afford the cherished privacy it provides.

More formal cut-stone walls can also look very romantic when they have had time to

A careful combination of natural-looking planting and man-made barriers can turn any garden into a private haven, secluded from the outside world. It doesn't take very long for a vigorous climber like Actinidia kolomikta *to soften and improve the feeling of sanctuary provided by a solid stone wall. Having scaled the wall, its slender stems will arch back toward the ground to make a partial light canopy, which can be used to offer a comforting feeling of enclosure above a seat. Tall plants flanking such a seat, like the euphorbias here, will always reinforce that feeling.*

develop a patina of moss and lichen. Because quarrying the stones involves skilled labor, such walls are usually more expensive than random-coursed walls, although finding someone to build them may be easier, as the work involves similar techniques to those used in bricklaying.

Much of the charm of genuine stone walls can be obtained at less cost if they are built of cement-based reconstituted stone. They never weather as convincingly, but modern manufacturing methods make them quite acceptable in appearance. Such blocks are usually available with either a smooth surface or a more rustic chiseled finish. The better manufacturers ensure that each batch delivered contains a good selection of stones from different molds, to avoid too regular a look to the finished wall. Do not use the prefabricated blocks made to look like a section of a wall – it is impossible to make them look natural and they do not weather and age convincingly.

When a stone wall is being constructed, the mortar should be finished to lie deeper than the surface of the stone, giving an immediate effect of age. Pockets can be left, as the wall is constructed, in which you can establish trailing plants. An attractive combination of foliage and masonry can be achieved easily and seems more appropriate – and softer – than a bland vertical surface.

Very attractive walls can be made from large beach boulders. When set together in mortar, their curved surfaces leave plenty of potential for the creation of planting pockets. Alternatively, and to prevent too much mortar being exposed to the weather, informal patterns of sea shells or fragments of terracotta can be pressed into the mortar before it hardens.

The best of new bricks, even those labeled 'antique finish' take a great many years to develop a look of maturity. Romantic gardeners are therefore obliged to seek out, and frequently pay dear for, genuine old bricks with which to build their walls. The thriving trade in demoli-

RIGHT *High walls of old soft-colored brick make beautifully romantic barriers. Of course they should never be left entirely bare but, as here, have pretty climbers, like roses and honeysuckle, growing over them and well-shaped wall plants set against them. Here the elegantly shaped topiary sentinels of evergreen boxwood,* Buxus sempervirens, *are seen to particularly good effect against the brick.*

LEFT *Surrounding the garden with walls of old, irregularly shaped stone is perhaps the most romantic way of excluding the outside world. When, as here, the wall is weathered, buttressed, overhung with ivy and climbing roses and penetrated by a Gothic arched doorway and a simple wooden door, the effect is perfect.*

tion materials is now making this easier than it has been. Some of the best, natural-colored softer bricks will often have lost a lot of their mechanical strength over the years, and this can create problems where walls of 2.5m/8ft or more are required, since no one will want to build a high wall entirely of old bricks of dubious strength. One technique to overcome this is to incorporate buttresses into the wall, where there is sufficient room, which can create something of a medieval air. If there is no one to object to a rather unpleasing outside face, a cheaper solution is to construct the wall of plain concrete blocks, faced on the inside only with old bricks. From within the garden, provided that the pointing has been carefully carried out, the wall will soon seem as mellow as any which might have stood in its place for a century or more.

FENCES

If you do not have, and cannot afford, high walls around your garden, you will have to choose from among the many types of fencing available. The most natural-looking is rough-cut lumber, overlapped and fastened to stout posts. This can be very difficult to find, but is often available from sawmills. You can determine the degree of rusticity you find acceptable by selecting either split tree trunks with the bark still in place and the branches merely lopped off, or rough-sawn debarked lengths of wood, which will give a more finished look and which can, of course, be stained to a more suitable soft color to mask their rawness.

Provided they are set on the outside of the fence and cannot be seen from the garden,

CANE FENCING
The life of garden fencing made from whole canes or bamboo can be extended by making them double sided.

A SPLIT-LOG FENCE
The life of fences made from split logs can be greatly extended if they are attached to strong wooden rails linking concrete posts well bedded into the ground. These will not rot and, provided the log sections are supported above soil level, the fence will last in good repair for many years.

concrete posts set firmly in concrete footings and linked by wooden cross-members make excellent supports for fencing lumber. Even if the lumber is dipped in preservative or impregnated in a vacuum tank, fences of this type will not last for ever, but they should survive for ten years or more, which is long enough to allow plants established just inside them to mature enough to take over their screening role. Meanwhile, as they are made of wood it is an easy matter to attach climbing plants to them.

If your only recourse is to the standard modular larchlap or closeboard fencing panels which are readily available, then stain them to reduce their raw new look and coat them with preservative to prolong their relatively short lives. Then fasten wires along them to encourage climbers to smother and disguise them and, if you have the space, plant a belt of trees and shrubs in front of them.

Very attractive soft-looking fences can be made from rolls of either whole or split bamboo canes or some of the taller grasses. Their durability is very variable: the split grass rolls deteriorate very quickly and in windy areas will only last about two years. Whole grass or bamboo is tougher, with a life determined largely by the gauge and quality of the binding wire. In either case the material should be firmly supported. Here, as usual, the more expensive

ABOVE The wire-link fence on the right provides a wonderful support for a mass of climbing roses, which in turn help to hide its presence as does the dense drift of herbaceous plants at its feet. Complete masking can be provided by quick-growing evergreen climbers, like ivy.

(in mild areas) will accomplish this task within three years, provided you ensure that their delicate new stems are not damaged. Do not attach them directly to the fence but instead tie them in with hemp twine to bamboo canes wired to the chainlink or netting.

Rapid temporary screening will result from a combination of Russian vine *(Polygonum bald-schuanicum)* on the fence and tall, fast-growing grasses in front of it. Try *Miscanthus, Erianthus ravennae,* or *Cortaderia* species, which have dry stems which persist for most of the winter to act as a softening screen. They can, however, only be used where there is plenty of space, since as they mature, they do form substantial clumps. In milder, moister areas, some of the larger bamboos, such as *Pseudosasa japonica,* could be used in place of the grasses.

HEDGES

Tall thick hedges of evergreen shrubs and trees provide a marvelous shelter from the outside world and a filtering of sound and wind. In a rural setting they can even seem more appropriate than a high wall. Junipers, arbor-vitae, hollies and even the common but wonderfully fast-growing × *Cupressocyparis leylandii* can be used for this work. Boxwood and yew have traditionally been used to form thick buttresses and impenetrable hedges, and do much to provide that sense of age-old calm that is such an important feature of the romantic garden; perhaps their small leaf and close texture contribute to this effect.

Deciduous tree species such as European hornbeam, *Carpinus betulus,* are fast growing and will provide a reasonable hedge framework within about three years, retaining their bronzed leaves even in winter to provide a semblance of leaf cover.

It must be said that, if it usually takes up to five years to make a hedge 2m/6ft high, creating a hedge tall enough to exclude the world effectively takes time and patience – so a man-made barrier may well be necessary.

the product the longer it is likely to last. In general it must be said that fences of these materials offer a temporary screening solution and should only be used in a sheltered situation.

For anyone prepared to tolerate a surrounding that looks unattractive for the first three years, a chainlink fence offers a secure, high barrier. If attached to steel posts, like those used for tennis court surroundings, chainlink will provide a good support for quick-growing evergreen climbers which will rapidly conceal its harsh man-made look. Very strong wire netting can be used in a similar way, although it is not so secure. Such plants as *Clematis armandii,* English ivy *(Hedera helix)* or *Trachelospermum jasminoides*

IMPROVING THE BOUNDARY

In many instances the romantic gardener will take over a garden in which the boundaries will be incomplete, for one reason or another; perhaps decay, possibly because the previous owners enjoyed the view and did not wish to obscure it.

If the garden is already surrounded by a mature but low wall, a sense of seclusion may be achieved by increasing its height. A very quick way of doing this is to attach strong posts to the outside vertical surface, with screws and plugs, using them to support either trellis panels or swags of rope over which climbers can be trained above wall level.

Attempts to complete an enclosing wall by marrying new masonry to old, even of the same type, are usually only too obvious. It is often better to change the texture and appearance of the wall (though not the height) by using brick to complete gaps in a stone surrounding, or stone where the existing wall is of brick. This can look as if you have deliberately chosen to add variety to the surface and the difference in age will be less obvious.

With brick walls, this problem can also be reduced by the careful selection of matching secondhand bricks. Weathering will still take some time to reproduce a satisfactory blending of old and new, but the texture and color will be similar. Do ensure that details of mortaring and bonding are carried through from old to new, and that attention is paid to matching the coping, whether it is of brick on edge, tiles or other materials. The new section of wall can be coated with milk, yogurt or cow slurry to promote the rapid development of moss and lichen. These will quickly provide the ancient, established air required.

Very often the romantic gardener will be faced with a hedge that forms an incomplete screen. Individual hedge plants may have died or been uprooted in a storm, and establishing new plants to take their place can be difficult. Space and water are needed by all in the hedgerow, and

ABOVE *Cleverly positioned thickly planted trees and shrubs have been used to hide the boundaries of this garden and divide it into a series of leafy glades.*

LEFT *The height of the boundary wall of this garden has been increased to provide greater privacy and seclusion by attaching beautiful trellis panels to it, and using the trellis to support climbing plants. This creates a wonderfully intimate site for a simple seat.*

competition will be intense. Newcomers should be very well fed and watered during their first two seasons. Plenty of space for their roots should be created by digging extra deep and wide planting holes and carefully cutting through and removing some roots of adjacent plants, which will suffer only a temporary setback.

DISGUISING THE BOUNDARIES

Excluding the world by erecting a high fence, wall or hedge round the boundary, while essential in most situations, brings its own problems. Ideally, a romantic garden should also seem totally boundless, while a high boundary is difficult to disguise.

If the garden is small, much can be done by clothing it with climbing plants and wall shrubs. Several methods of attaching plants to the wall or fence can be used, and should be tailored to suit the growth of the plants you have selected – some will need no support at all.

Wire strands and trellis can be attached to brick or stone walls and wooden fences of sturdy construction, and will offer support to climbing roses, clematis and honeysuckles. The self-clinging *Hydrangea petiolaris* and *Hedera* species need no support, just guidance in their youth, and nor do the pretty *Parthenocissus* and *Vitis* species. Always plant away from the dry base of a wall or fence so that plants can make use of natural rainfall. They can be trained in toward the support with canes and hemp twine.

Evergreen wall shrubs can also be used for masking. *Pyracantha* specimens are extremely hardy and tolerant, rewarding you with flowers and berries, responding well to shearing to shape. Wall shrubs can also host intertwining clematis or honeysuckle. Similarly, vigorous climbers, such as *Clematis montana* in its various shades can be used to grow through dark yew or holly hedges. The froth of foliage and flower emerging on the surface of the hedge offers an exciting visual treat.

In larger gardens, a good way of disguising the boundaries is to plant a belt of rapid-growing evergreen trees and shrubs just inside the boundary When they have established themselves, stretches of leafy wall or fence will simply be seen as a romantic green haze through the foliage of shrub and tree. Trees and shrubs whose branches tend toward the horizontal, or even arch and droop like the Canadian hemlock, *Tsuga canadensis*, or *Chamaecyparis nootkatensis* 'Pendula' are particularly effective in masking a wall. The eye will follow the line of their fronds and attention will be distracted from the lines of the wall or fence behind. This effect can be reinforced by planting in front of them a mixture

LEFT *The house is usually the largest feature that can be seen from inside the garden, and the treatment of its facade must be carefully considered if it isn't to destroy the romantic mood. Here, what was clearly already a most attractive property has been embellished with climbing plants to soften its walls. Climbers have been allowed to cover the tree trunk too, linking it to the house and hence making the house seem a natural part of the garden.*

of evergreen and deciduous shrubs and smaller trees with as many varied foliage types as possible. Light reflects back in different ways from the dark shiny oval leaves of camellias and rhododendrons, the pale green lacy foliage of honeylocust, *Gleditsia triacanthos*, or golden leaf elderberry, *Sambucus racemosa* 'Plumosa Aurea'. When these plants are mixed, the eye finds it difficult to penetrate such a gauzy screen.

Ideally the boundaries will come to form merely a green backdrop to the exciting and interesting details of the garden itself. It is vital, not only that no one should be able to see into the garden, but also that the garden itself should not be entirely visible at first glance. Mystery and imagination go hand in hand, and must be encouraged by every means at your disposal. This theme will be expanded in the next chapter.

THE HOUSE IN THE GARDEN

There is little doubt that some gardens could be made more romantic if the house were to be disguised in some way, although you may well be fortunate enough to occupy a house with an attractive garden facade. However, even if you have to regard the garden side of the house as a challenge, much can be done to mask its worst defects. Unattractive windows can be provided with shutters – or even with Gothic decoration, if this would be in keeping – while whole ground floors can be swallowed up by a pergola or veranda.

It is harder to deal with higher stories, but one answer is to clothe them with decorative trellis-work which, if thoughtfully planned, can be very attractive. It can also act as a support for the exceptionally beautiful *Wisteria* with its wonderful drooping racemes of mauve or white or even purple flowers in early summer, or the blazing autumn glory of the Virginia creeper, *Parthenocissus quinquefolia*. This latter will happily clothe a house without visible means of support, should you prefer this.

For generations experts have inveighed against allowing ivy to creep up house walls. It is undeniably romantic, however, and is unlikely to damage masonry which is well pointed and in good condition. However, it is important to prevent vigorous climbers from creeping under the eaves, into gutters or between roof tiles, once they reach roof height. This will entail some ladderwork each season to cut away all the high-leading shoots.

A house which, ungarnished, already has an old-world appeal, requires less cosmetic attention. Often as little as a simple metal or wooden trellis archway supporting festoons of climbing roses will provide as romantic an introduction to the garden as anyone could need.

THE ENTRANCE TO THE GARDEN

The entrance to a garden is like the foyer of a theater – it begins to set the mood for the whole experience. If you have a separate entrance to your garden it can have a greater impact than many features discovered later in the tour of the garden. You must therefore ensure that the gateways and doorways induce as romantic a feeling as possible.

They should be, above all, irresistibly inviting. A sense of mystery should not be marred by any sense of exclusion – visitors should be totally engulfed by the romantic garden. This encouragement to enter can be augmented by making the door surrounding as attractive as possible. The notion that a door conveys any suggestion of prohibition is immediately swept away if it is surrounded by John Keats' 'fragrant

censers swinging light in air' in the form of climbing roses and summer jasmine.

In many cases, doorways and gateways are used so frequently and unthinkingly that you tend to ignore them. Sometimes they will be charming features worth preserving unaltered; frequently their ordinariness will, for visitors with fresh eyes, shatter the very illusion you are trying to create. It is, of course, also vitally important that they look just as romantic from within the garden.

When starting afresh, the actual form of the door can be a matter of choice. Arched rather

A ROMANTIC INTRODUCTION
A rustic wooden arch supporting a climbing rose can be very effective in increasing the romantic feeling of a doorway. Using boxwood trelliswork or welded iron rod to make the archway can be equally attractive. Simple trellis panels attached to the walls and linked above the doorway provide a cheap and alluring alternative.

25

than square-topped doors are more attractive, while pointed Gothic arches always seem more romantic than semicircular Roman arches, as long as they are in keeping with the surrounding architecture. More expensive, but beautiful when weathered, are cut or cast stone door surroundings – such embellishments suggest, subliminally, that the garden is part of a world in which no unpleasant economic restraints exist.

Very often the effect of a good-looking gateway is destroyed because insufficient atten-

ROMANTIC DOORWAYS
AND GATEWAYS
Entrances can set the mood for the whole garden visit, so they should be as attractive as possible. Gothic arches always seem more romantic than plain square or rounded ones. Nondescript entrances can often be successfully embellished by surrounding them with stone-work acquired from demolition sites. Attention should be paid to the quality and appearance of the door itself. Tall ironwork gates should be given substantial wooden or masonry supports.

26

tion is paid to the gate or door itself. The greatest offenders are overfinished, loudly painted wooden doors with unattractive mass-produced hinges and latches. Doors of thick, broad planks, whose surface is not too finely finished, simply colored with one of the range of delightful pale stains now available, look best. As the stain fades the wood weathers to a fine dull ashen silver with just a trace of color. Heavy doors of this type need solid-looking ironwork to match. If a 'see-through' gate rather than a solid door is required, there are plenty of companies who offer wrought iron gates in all shapes and sizes. Unless the quality of the decoration is of a very high standard, the rule in selection should be the plainer the better.

Existing arched doorways usually need little to increase their natural attractiveness. If, however, you have rather a plain square-topped door, a great deal can be done to enhance it. Solid wooden doors of good quality can be stripped of paint and stained to a suitably mellow shade, and better ironwork can be fitted. Or, if appropriate, the door can be replaced with an iron gate. The framework of simple rectangular doorways can be improved by using good wooden moldings, or even half-round lumber if a rustic look is in keeping.

Alternatively, an ordinary gateway can be given a 'green porch'. It may take time to achieve the ancient boxwood or yew bastion that can occasionally be seen, but an arch of trellis or ironwork will be smothered by climbers within a growing season or two. When an evergreen honeysuckle or climbing rose becomes established, the door itself will be largely hidden and the eye distracted from it.

Once the garden has been entered, the sense of having gained a sanctuary should steal over you. You have established your garden frame – the green impenetrable boundary – and now the visitor is drawn inexorably toward the romance and secrets within. In gardening, as in other decorative arts, compositional weaknesses can often be overcome by providing screens or distractions. Structures or large plants inside the garden can be sited to make a direct view of the boundary difficult. Or, more subtly, attention can be diverted from the perimeter by the commanding presence of a feature such as a pergola or obelisk, or even just an attractive seat or a particularly noteworthy plant strategically placed. Above all the romantic garden must be self-contained, almost inward looking, and a voyage round it should not destroy the initial sense of mystery and surprise.

A SIMPLE GATE
Gates in low walls can look rather fussy, and the simplest designs are the most satisfactory. To give them more stature and emphasize their importance as a barrier to be crossed before entering a new area of the garden, they can be topped with an archway of trellis or welded iron supporting climbing plants.

AN EXOTIC GARDEN

*In this tropical-looking sanctuary, a stone vase adds
intrigue to a shady corner as it hides behind the fronds of
a palmetto and the variegated ginger it houses. The
semiformal brick paving (right) does not detract from the
romantic atmosphere created by the profuse vegetation.
The tendril-like structure of the wire chairs harmonizes
beautifully with the surroundings.*

Hot, humid places might be uncomfortable to work in during the stickier periods of the year, but they can be a paradise for gardeners; in a generally moist, warm climate, plants grow at an amazing rate, sometimes too quickly. These types of conditions particularly suit subtropical plants, whose exotic, often architectural, forms have such outstanding character that they always command attention. Massed together, they quickly convert any corner into the sort of primitive Eden that Gauguin so loved to paint.

This garden, which measures only 18m/60ft by 6m/20ft, is attached to a city house, and its owner has converted what is really only a small plot into an almost overwhelmingly plant-filled romantic place. It is amazing just how much variety and interest it is possible to pack into such an awkward site as this.

From the brick patio by the house there is a choice of routes down the garden, each offering different vistas and both converging on a second seating area away from the heat-retaining mass of the structure of the building itself. Here you find cooler, airy conditions – like a welcoming embrace on those still, humid evenings.

Within the garden are two water features – a well on the patio and a pool that is almost completely covered with succulent-looking water lettuce. Two water features are not ostentation in an area such as this, since the water table is extremely high and you don't have to dig down far to find water. In fact, the paths in this garden had to be given a particularly deep rubble base to raise them up on to dry, stable land.

The garden terminates in a somewhat forbidding, but characterful, old brick convent wall that rises like a cliff face to 4.5m/15ft above the garden. Approximately half of its surface area is hidden behind an attractive, thin-sparred, lean-to

Built to provide winter shelter for tender, tropical plants, this lean-to glasshouse does another useful job in largely banishing from view a rather forbidding brick wall at the end of the garden. Easy access through the marshy ground the garden has been built on is provided by a pathway of stone slabs.

glasshouse, which is used to protect the truly tropical plants that require some extra cosseting to thrive during the slightly cooler winter months. Much of the rest of the wall is masked by a glorious profusion of vegetation, including the upwardly thrusting *Phoenix* palms and robust plantains. Wall surfaces inside the glasshouse are well masked with rampant creepers such as merliton vine.

The need for heavy shade on hot days has been fulfilled by planting trees, such as hollies, magnolias, avocados, lemons and laurels, making the light in some areas of the garden mysterious and subdued. Seen from beneath their canopy, the bright, flowering plants seem all the more startling in contrast. Notable among them, and soaring to 4.5m/15ft and more, are the pale-green-leaved cassias holding up their yellow, candelabra heads, tufty clumps of tall, grass-leaved liriopes and hemerocallis, white-trumpeted crinums and beautiful butterfly gingers. Benefiting from some shade, azaleas in tubs are provided with the acidic peaty compost they really need to thrive.

Most people believe that Elysium is a place that effortlessly supplies all that one needs for survival. It is not surprising, therefore, that in this garden vegetables and herbs jostle with flowering plants for space and light.

Polished, purple egg plants the size of small pineapples compete for recognition as being among the handsomest of plants; bright yellow daisies of Jerusalem artichoke shine out like carnival lanterns; and kale and broccoli glory in the moist soil that all leaf vegetables and brassicas relish. Basil, mint and parsley all contribute their fragrant aromas to an air already heavy with the scent of lemon blossoms, while wild strawberries make an attractive as well as mouth-watering ground cover.

To prevent the whole atmosphere of the garden becoming too opulent and full, its owner has wisely used spiky architectural plants, such as cycads and sago palms, to provide that all-essential excitement and contrast.

PLANT LIST

POND, SURROUNDING & SEATING AREA
Prunus laurocerasus
Citrus limon
Phoenix dactylifera
Musa × paradisiaca
Merliton vine
Montbretia
Cassia alata
Iris spp.
Ferns
Pistia stratiotes
Hibiscus rosa-sinensis
Cycas revoluta
Olea europea
Nandina domestica
Liriope muscari
Magnolia virginiana
Viola spp.

VEGETABLE GARDEN
Peach tree
Plum tree
Seasonal vegetables incl. eggplant, Jerusalem artichoke, kale, broccoli, asparagus, basil, mint, parsley, wild strawberry

BRICK PATIOS
Hydrangea cvs.
Petargonium spp., cvs.
Camellia
Althaea rosea
Ilex (as screen)
Hemerocallis spp.
Crinum bulbispermum
Cassia splendens
Musa acaminata
Rhododendron spp.
Zingiber officinale
Impatiens
Lilium spp.
Aspidistra
Persea americana

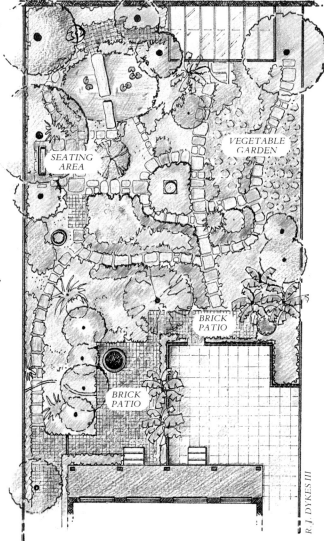

VEGETABLE GARDEN

SEATING AREA

BRICK PATIO

BRICK PATIO

R. J. DYKES III

A SECRET GARDEN

*In this secluded garden, shrubby copses edged with outstanding plants
enclose and project into what was once a plain, rectangular lawn. Now there
are separate secret areas beyond, and a well-placed garden seat has been used
as a lure to encourage visitors to investigate further. A crossing of paths
(right) is luxuriant with foliage, including four sentinel 'Sky Rocket'
junipers. The path is kept narrow to enhance its secret romantic quality.*

This transformation of an open, rectangular plot into an enchanting, secret garden demonstrates triumphantly how, with good planning and thoughtful planting, something as unpromising as a bald acre of alkaline clay soil in a wind-blasted situation can be made to seem at once expansive and rambling yet enclosed as the cloisters of a monastery.

In the beginning, the major area of the garden was a large lawn flanked by herbaceous beds. The best asset was an old farm pond beyond the lawn. The first task was the planting of an evergreen shelter belt of pines, Lawson cypress, holm oak and blue cedar to minimize the effects of cold easterly winds. Surprisingly, many *Cupressus macrocarpa*, which, theoretically, should not have tolerated such cold conditions, were also planted in quantity and have thrived.

This evergreen barrier was reinforced by a thick planting of deciduous trees and shrubs. Apart from additional shelter, these trees offer wonderful cover for snowdrops, bluebells, cyclamen and the occasional martagon lilies that edge the paths through the garden.

Copses of shrubs and trees projecting into the lawn have been used to break up the former, formal arrangement and to create mysterious, unseen areas that need to be entered to be appreciated. Skirting the wedge-shaped copse projecting into the eastern margin of the lawn, plants with a generally green coloration, such as hellebores, euphorbias and nicotianas, dominate.

In the largest copse breaking up one edge of the lawn, the emphasis is on the orange and scarlet colors of shrub roses and plants such as crocosmias, lychnis and cheiranthus. These can be seen against an evergreen backdrop of shrubs and trees, including boxwood, laurel and bay.

A major feature of the site is a north/south pathway running through the copse and offering

Canopies of foliage form natural tunnels and throw the brightness of the open glades beyond into starker contrast.

Although formal slabs have been used for the path, they appear quite romantic in a wild garden.

a vista from the middle of the house to the pond. This is bordered by a glorious combination of herbaceous plants and shrubs, including roses, sheared *Osmanthus burkwoodii*, purple-leaved *Prunus*, tall *Senecio greyii*, spiraeas, saxifrage, bluebells, tulips and honesty, spilling over onto the edges and breaking up any hard lines. Here, the plants press in close enough to give the feeling that you are almost being caressed.

This main route through the garden is crossed by another path, which was opened to create a view from the center of the lawn through to a fountain stationed in a lily pond in an enclosed area of the garden. Four erect 'Sky Rocket' junipers make the crossing of the paths a glorious focal point. Plants with white, silver and gray flowers and foliage predominate in the lily pool garden, and privacy is well assured by a hedge of tall *Lonicera nitida*.

To the west of the white and silver garden is a large area penetrated by brick-paved paths through a planting in which blues, purples and pale yellows are emphasized. Scillas, forget-me-nots, phlox, eryngiums, agapanthus, aconites, sisyrinchiums, scabious and tulips all jostle for attention.

North of this area is a genuinely wild garden with rough grass, wild flowers and naturalized bulbs. This area is divided diagonally by pretty paved paths of slabs set in diamond shapes bedded in gravel.

Embodied in the making of this garden are the principles to which its designer always tries to adhere. All the boundaries, for example, are 'blurred' with evergreens and shrubs in an effort to highlight a real sense of mystery. Another important principle is that features that make solid, transverse lines across the field of vision are shunned. Instead, if unavoidable, they are broken up in some way, either by arranging to place a visually diverting feature in front of them or by making a gap leading to another garden 'room'. In general, color harmonies are stressed rather than jarring contrasts and, wherever possible, bold but gentle curves are employed.

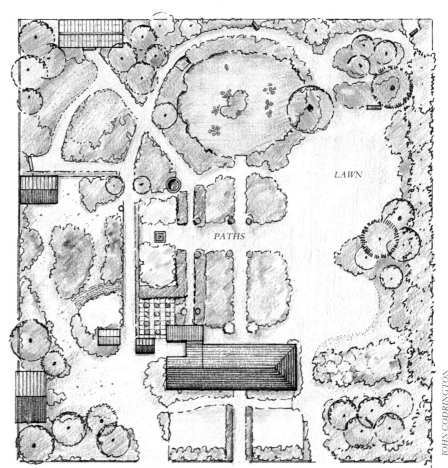

LAWN

PATHS

JOHN CODRINGTON

PLANT LIST

SURROUNDING TREES & WOOD
Populus spp.
Cupressus macrocarpa
Chamaecyparis lawsoniana
Quercus ilex
Cedrus atlantica 'Glauca'
Ilex spp.
Corylus avellana
Galanthus nivalis
Endymion nonscriptus
Cyclamen spp.
Lilium martagon

POND SURROUNDING
Salix × chrysocoma
Rheum palmatum
Iris spp.
Inula afghanica
Rodgersia pinnata
Heracleum mantegazzanium

PATHS
Juniperus 'Sky Rocket'
Rosa spp.
Osmanthus burkwoodi
Prunus cerasifera 'Pissardii'
Senecio greyi
Spiraea
Saxifraga
Endymion nonscriptus
Tulipa spp.
Lunaria
Lonicera nitida

LAWN SURROUNDING
Buxus sempervirens
Prunus laurocerasus
Laurus nobilis
Helleborus spp.
Nicotiana
Euphorbia
Crocosmia
Lychnis
Cheiranthus

WEST SIDE
Scilla
Myosotis
Phlox
Eryngium
Agapanthus
Aconitum
Sisyrinchium striatum
Scabiosa

ROMANCE
WITHIN

appy is the gardener with the good fortune to have high, mossy walls enclosing lush beds of greenery studded with fragrant flowers, with paths meandering through groves of trees into sunlit glades or around a tranquil pool. Most of us, however, will have to work quite hard initially to achieve similar effects. Nevertheless, with care it is possible to transform a bare site or a neat, open plot into a place that is secluded and redolent with atmosphere. Romantic gardens, attempting as they do to offer a glamorized version of untrammeled nature, will never win prizes for tidiness; they are, however, always intriguing because all their features are not overt. They guard their secrets closely, while hinting at what they have to offer with enticing glimpses through partial barriers – archways, pergolas, screens of trellis or foliage or gaps in solid barriers like dividing walls.

In an established but open garden there will be much that is worth preserving – especially, well-grown examples of beautiful shrubs and trees. You should note their position and include them as important features – together with the other immutables such as boundaries, aspect, soil and climatic conditions – that have to be considered when designing or remodeling the garden to make it more interesting. The sense of mystery and interest that you are striving for is primarily aroused by ensuring that the whole garden is never visible at a glance. This will be possible even in the smallest garden by building screens at right angles to the boundaries so that what lies beyond is concealed at first sight.

When planning such a garden, it is important to have a strong and clear overall structure within which the planting for luxuriant, enclosing effects and the placing of romantic features can be set. Aim to divide even the smallest garden into distinct areas that are isolated from each other by built or planted barriers. A sense of movement is essential; a natural flow through the garden will lure you to return and wander again through its delights.

SECRET CAVERNS OF FOLIAGE

A good idea is to plan the garden as a series of leafy glades with heavily shaded margins and brighter centers, connected by meandering paths that are always disappearing around foliage screens. Siting these glades and determining the route of paths – and hence seeing where dividing trees and shrubs should be planted or other screens built – should be worked out on a scale plan of the garden. Points to remember are the ultimate spread of trees, that paths of less than 60cm/2ft wide are uncomfortably cramped and that glades of less than 2.5m/8ft across will be insignificant. Young trees will need an area around their trunks kept clear of grass or weeds until they are well established. The fact that plants will try to fill the space available should not be forgotten. Remember, however, that an overplanted garden is likely to be much more romantic than one where sparse plants stand out like sentinels. It is also easier to remove un-

In a most atmospheric setting, a flower-filled leafy glade is approached through a dark rocky passage. Such beautifully framed vistas are quintessential to a romantic garden, because they provide a touch of darkness and mystery and lure the visitor forward with glimpses of color and light.

wanted plants – even the rapidly growing coarser trees – than it is to obtain that feeling of leafy abundance without dense planting.

One way to create a leafy cavern is almost to surround an open central area with an irregular ring of mostly evergreen trees, such as holm oak, yew, cypress or holly. The larger the garden the greater the number of caverns that can be created, the longer the glades can be and the thicker the stands of trees that divide them. The paths through such gardens should be set among these stands, so that walking along them offers the sensation of walking in woodland.

In many city gardens there will be room for only one reasonably sized leafy cavern, set somewhere in the middle ground. On such a site, careful planting should create a dark screen near the house and against the far boundary, with the lighter glade at the center. However, to be effective and create a sense of drama, the varieties chosen to act as leafy dividers should still, ultimately, grow tall enough to make it necessary to look up toward their crowns against the sky. We might enjoy, but are unlikely to be impressed by, plants we can look down on. Fastigiate trees such as eastern red cedar, *Juniperus virginiana* 'Canaerti', upright English oak, *Quercus robur* 'Fastigiata', or western arbor-vitae, *Thuja plicata* 'Fastigiata', will give height without undue bulk.

Unity confers a sense of repose and tranquility; a more restful effect will be created by planting a grove of six European white birches than by dotting about individual trees of every color you can buy. Not only color needs consideration – the structure, leaf shape and texture, bark contrasts and spatial relationships of trees are important, as well as the more obvious grouping together of trees that enjoy the same soil and climatic conditions. This sense of unity is even more important in the small garden, where a successful effect will be created by keeping to just one species – using, perhaps yew or hornbeam alone, or perhaps a single variety of shrub rose, such as *Rosa alba* 'Celeste', to create a colorful screen.

— A SMALL ROMANTIC GARDEN —

FEATURES

1 Trellis obelisks planted with climbing roses
2 Mask trickling water into cantilevered stone basin
3 Planted trellis screen
4 Planted pergola
5 Framed vase on plinth in blind archway backed by mirror
6 Stone column on octagonal base supporting crystal orb
7 Shady arbor
8 Niche-type grotto planted with ferns etc.
9 Lily pool with marsh plants in part of surround
10 False doorway
11 Simple iron rod temple planted with climbers

PLANTING

Flowering evergreen shrub and herbaceous plant

Fragrant shrub rose

Fastigiate juniper

Prunus lusitanica

Quercus ilex

Pyrus salicifolia 'Pendula'

Viburnum tinus

Liliodendron tulipifera

Primula meadow

This city garden is 10m/33ft by 6.5m/21ft and surrounded by brick walls topped with trellis. On the terrace is a small wall-mounted water feature, and a concentration of old shrub roses and mound-forming aromatic plants with climbing roses on trellis obelisks. Intriguing views lead through the arch and along the pergola to the mirror-backed vase beyond. From the far end of the pergola a further lure is the crystal orb seen through a masonry arch. A diversion is provided by the primula meadow glade and the arbor, half-hidden by the evergreen hedge. Turning the corner of the ruined wall reveals the climber-clad iron 'temple' and a false gateway, a secluded seat and view across the iris and lily meadow to the waterlily pond. The garden is heavily planted with small-scaled trees.

Nothofagus dombeyi

Holly

2m/6½ft tall semi-formal evergreen hedge

Picea breweriana

Prunus laurocerasus

Cupressus arizonica

Meadow of several types of iris, lilies, sisyrhinchium, etc.

Gleditsia triacanthos

Prunus subhirtella

Taxus baccata

SURFACES

Semiformal paving in old brick or weathered stone, inset with attractive mound-forming plants like thymes, dianthus etc.

Grit surfacing

The view from the terrace through the pergola and trellis screen permits enticing glimpses of the garden beyond, and a vase in a distant alcove lures the eye.

From the crystal orb, two quite different vistas – to the temple, and through the ruined archway – make the garden seem extensive, and the reflection in the mirror-backed false gateway make that vista seem endless. An exploration reveals the arbor and primula meadow behind the hedge.

– A LARGE ROMANTIC GARDEN –

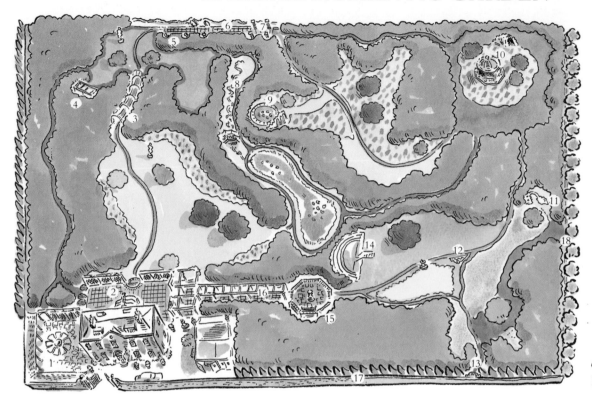

11 Relic corner of ruined building with archway

12 Relic Roman pavement set in grit path

13 Dribble fountain in alcove

14 Excavated 'natural' theater, stone facing to seats, miniature thymes on sitting surface

15 Seat backed by stone wall planted with trailing plants

16 Planted pergola

17 Existing old brick wall made good

18 Existing high stone wall

PLANTING

Mixed deciduous/ evergreen tree and shrub planting with taller and larger trees in the middle of the plantations, edged with lower shrubs melded in with larger perennial herbaceous plants; along path edges many woodland bulbs and herbaceous plants

Conceived for a 6000 sq m/ 1½ acre site, this garden offers two distinct types of experience. The minor paths go through woodland only, while the major paths and alleys lead to a series of glades. The first has a tight mown lawn, edged with mixed shrubs and herbaceous beds and ornamental trees. A planted tunnel leads to the second glade, with a lavender lawn and arbor. From here, a paved alley runs between a planted ruined wall and a sheared hedge pierced by openings containing sculpture busts. In glade three, a mown path through a wildflower meadow leads to a Gothic ruined wall and a raised stone-edged lily pond. In the fourth glade the charm of the raised octagonal temple contrasts with the dark grotto behind the mount. The final glade contains an amphitheater and a primula meadow. An octagonal court and paved pergola lead to the house, and the heart of the woodland has a rill and pond with moss lawn edges.

FEATURES

1 Open-sided arcade and double-sided trellis wall with yew growing inside, surrounding paved yard with central herb beds and ornamental central planted urn

2 Double trellis screen planted with climbers, with arch over concave/ convex stone steps

3 Curved planted tunnel

4 Planted arbor

5 Busts on columns

6 Semiruined heavily planted stone wall with ferns and a water basin in an alcove

7 Stone pillars with climbing roses

8 Rocky cairn, from which spring spills into cobble-bottomed rill leading to pond with moss lawn and marsh banks

9 Raised lily pond in 76cm/ 30in high formal stone wall becoming decrepit, with chipped cope-stones and dianthus growing in cracks; single white water lily in water; ruined wall with Gothic windows rising to 2.7m/ 9ft in places with integral stone seat on pool side

10 Octagonal temple on mount with grotto below

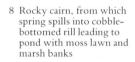
Smooth mown lawn

Magnolia grandiflora

Fragrant shrub rose

Prunus subhirtella

Quercus ilex

Herbaceous/small shrub mixed beds

Lavender lawn

Flower meadow lawn

Mixed ground cover of dwarf types, ajugas, very low junipes, procumbent rosemary and some mound-formers like iceplants and ballotas on coarse gravel

Drifts of close-planted lily, iris, hemerocallis, agapanthus

Primula meadow

Meadow of mixed tufty ornamental grasses

Wind screen of mixed *Prunus lusitanica*, *P. laurocerasus*, *Ilex* spp. and *Taxus baccata*

Screen of *Chamaecyparis lawsoniana*

SURFACES

Formal paving

Mixed stone slab and brick paving

Coarse grit, used for paving and 2m/6ft wide formal path

Informal bark-topped paths

Plenty of room in a well-drained part of the garden is required to make a convincing relic amphitheater like this, but if it is possible it can be one of the easiest follies to build. Earth excavated to make the bowl can be used to build mounds – perhaps for a gazebo or temple – elsewhere.

These busts on plinths, sited in alcoves in a tall evergreen hedge, add mystery and nobility to an enclosed walkway. Each few yards offers new interest in a stroll down the alley.

Few follies are more romantic than the simulated ruins of an old abbey, which can be made from cut stone arch, window or doorway components from Victorian buildings which are being demolished. Here they are sited by a lily pool whose stone margins are romantically displaced by invading plants.

RIGHT Even a freestanding iron arch wreathed in climbers can serve to provide a sense of division in a garden. Commanding the eye to linger, it absorbs attention and makes the observer wonder what might lie beyond.

—INTERNAL SCREENS—

If you cannot instantly provide the secrecy that your leafy caverns will offer in time, or if the garden is too small for such a grove, the solution is to build either temporary or permanent internal divisions. These will also provide a sense of direction and a motive for movement. The aim is to obscure partially or mask the view and to offer an enticement to see what lies beyond. If there is sufficient space, several screens could be used to make different 'rooms' within the garden. Archways within the screens can provide added enticement and a frame for the view beyond. Even in the smallest garden, partial screens placed at right angles to and built out from the side will create a sense of mystery by concealing parts of the garden from first view and determining a circuitous path through it. As a general rule, the smaller the garden the lighter in structure the screen should be.

TRELLIS

In any garden, but particularly in one where space is at a premium, quick and attractive screens can be made by erecting trellis paneling fitted to stout wooden posts. Trellis has the great advantage of providing immediate screening and wonderful high freestanding support for the climbing plants that are so essential in bringing a romantic feeling to the garden. Even before planting, trelliswork itself can bring a general feeling of delicacy and lightness, which contrasts beautifully with the more brooding mood fostered by dark evergreens and heavy stonework. It also acts as an imperfect veil, allowing much but

FAR RIGHT An internal screen of trellis panels held between pillars of old brick has been disguised with a climbing rose and Solanum crispum *'Glasnevin'. The latter is a wonderfully quick climber, with the advantage of remaining in leaf until late in the year.*

not all of what lies beyond to be seen. There is something which touches strange chords about a wall with a hundred windows which offer only a single view.

Debutant gardeners will probably buy the ready-made trellis panels, and indeed many of the more elaborate ones on offer, with Gothic arches or chinoiserie detailing, are very attractive. But before committing themselves, they should examine the product very carefully. To be sufficiently strong to support heavy climbers and resist high winds, trellis should be made of seasoned softwood at least 2.5×2.5cm/1×1in in section. Cadmium or zinc-plated countersunk screws will prevent corrosion. Many ready-made panels are offered in lighter-grade wood, simply nailed or stapled together, and will not last long. More experienced handy men and

TRELLIS SCREENS
Attractively designed trellis structures offer a pleasing effect immediately, which is enhanced as they are covered with climbers.

TRELLIS ARCHES
Trellis arches can be made out of thin pliable builders' lath wood. In turn, several strips coated with contact adhesive are pulled and held in place with wrenches round a curved shape consisting of nails hammered into a wooden board. When all the strips have been pressed together firmly to exclude air, the wrenches are removed and the laths remain curved.

women may try making trelliswork themselves – it is relatively simple.

While in some gardens white trellis will look well, subdued shades of brown, dark green or silvery blue can look very romantic. Curved trellis elements enable you to build more interesting screens, including archways, simply as decoration or over paths. In a small garden, walls lined with trellis arches give a hint of the monastery cloister. In tiny gardens, *trompe l'oeil* effects in trelliswork, sometimes combined with mirror glass, can deceive one's perceptions of the actual size of the garden very effectively.

WALLS

Internal walls will generally be lower than perimeter walls: something 2m/6½ft high will be adequate to prevent most people peering over. Constructed of materials which will blend well with both house and boundary walls, they should form part of a coherent design, carefully sited to lead the eye into and beyond the feature they delimit. They could, perhaps, form part of a ruined folly (see page 86). They may be straight or curved, solid or pierced, or perhaps serpentine, in which case they can be built of a single thickness of brick, whereas any other wall over

INTERNAL WALLS
Curved walls, incorporating old stone window surroundings to simulate ruins, make fine internal screens.

SOD WALL
The ancient Romans used inverted sods to make stretches of wall in districts where stone was scarce. Gardeners, too, can use the same technique to make internal walls or even attractive alcoves for seats.

RAISED BEDS
If peat blocks are used for low walls surrounding raised beds, which are also filled with peat, acid-loving plants can be grown in areas with alkaline soil.

1m/3ft high must be at least 23cm/9in wide. Old brick, with deep grouting, or stone will look attractive.

Whatever material is chosen, a deep planting trough along the top and planting pockets along the vertical surfaces should be incorporated. Suitable plants for these positions are alpines and rock plants and some low-growing shrubs – all those that thrive on low rainfall and have a naturally compact but sprawling habit. Choose from among the smaller campanulas, alpine phloxes and helianthemums.

Sometimes even lower partitions, such as raised beds, will give you the necessary sense of separation between two areas. These beds can be surrounded by brick, lumber or stone walls, but peat blocks offer perhaps the most romantic of all surroundings. On walls up to 50cm/18in high, they quickly become covered with moss and lichen and can be used directly as a foothold for plant roots which, once they become established, help to bind the peat blocks together. They look so beautiful and soft that it is sad that they are unsuitable for making higher structures.

Since the Romans built sections of Hadrian's Wall out of grass sods, there is no reason why someone with their own meadow should not do the same. Sods 7.5cm/3in thick are cut in slabs 30cm/1ft wide and 50cm/18in long and used to build walls which slope inward from base to apex. The sods are inverted as they are laid and after a few months their top and sides can be sheared tightly like a hedge, trimmed with a sickle, or allowed to develop unhindered. The latter is perhaps the best treatment for a romantic effect provided the wall does not become infested with bramble, nettles or thistles.

HEDGES

Planting a hedge is a good, but fairly slow, way of providing a leafy screen. Close-sheared evergreen hedges of boxwood, yew, holly or cypress, add stability and a sense of permanence. Deciduous hornbeam and beech can be used for a faster-growing hedge, but will look very sparse in winter for several years. A height of 2m/6½ft will be adequate, and you will have to wait some years to achieve it. Plant hedges only where you can make allowance for their ultimate width, too – a mature hedge of this height may be 1m/3ft wide at its base. More informal hedges can be created using flowering shrubs or shrub roses, which will give you flower and scent and a lovely unruliness but no leaf cover in the winter. Lower hedges still can be formed of fragrant lavender or rosemary.

PERGOLAS

Pergolas, made from strong columns linked transversally and longitudinally overhead, covered with a lush profusion of climbing plants, are wonderfully romantic features. They are important for providing internal structure in the garden – linking different areas and giving a strong vertical accent – as well as playing a screening role.

Pergolas based on substantial columns, perhaps the plastered rubble ones seen in Italy or the tile piers used by designers such as Lutyens, can make very attractive features even when unadorned. The heavier the columns, the

LEFT A pergola mounted on Tuscan Doric stone pillars is nobly festooned but somewhat wildly overgrown with climbers. This brings a slightly abandoned air of romance to the grandeur of the scene, which is echoed by the invasive plants softening the formality of the flight of steps and the placid pool.

weightier and more substantial the superstructure can be – a pleasing proportion is essential. Pergola columns should be spaced between 2m/6ft and 3m/9ft apart to avoid a feeling of claustrophobia. The top should be set at least 2.2m/7ft above the walkway to avoid any sense of oppression and to allow climbers to hang down unimpeded and unimpeding.

Their charm undoubtedly increases as the structure becomes masked, and this process can be aided by clothing the superstructure with coarse wire mesh. This will appear rather brash at first but will soon fade to a dull sheen and will hardly be noticed. A profusion of climbing roses and the leaves of the coignet grape, *Vitis coignetiae*, or the golden hop will all but obliterate the structure after just a few years. To extend the season of bloom, include a late-summer-flowering clematis like *C. tangutica*.

Walking through a pergola at certain times of day can have strangely disorientating effects. The movement from bright light through its pungent shadow and out into the brightness again produces a sense of surprise and an odd feeling of exposure, perhaps a little like surfacing from under water. By playing tricks of this kind the romantic gardener strives to manipulate perception and gently to persuade visitors to surrender to the garden's charm. A pergola is perhaps best placed near the start of the garden journey, to arouse us to the romance in store.

PLANTED TUNNELS

Similar in effect to pergolas, planted tunnels offer an alternative way of making a screen and creating a feeling of pleasing enclosure. Large arched hoops of metal are set at intervals over a path and linked longitudinally by spars of the same material. The leader stems of trees planted at their bases are trained upward, while the lateral branches are attached to run horizontally. When the leaders meet overhead, they can either be twined and allowed to go on growing or

ABOVE A simple pergola made out of turned wooden logs can look very effective when supporting plants like the young Actinidia kolomikta *in the foreground and several lovely* Wisteria sinensis *specimens planted at the feet of its columns. This superstructure is high enough to permit easy passage even when the climbers are in flower.*

PLANTED TUNNELS
Tubular steel arches linked
horizontally can be used to
make training frames for
plants set on both sides of
each hoop. When fully
grown the plants form
enchanting leafy tunnels.

SWAGS
Climbers are trained up
posts and then pruned to
encourage lateral branches to
develop, which are attached
to the suspended rope or
chain as they grow.

48

grafted together so as to become, in effect, a single plant with more than one root system. On meeting, horizontal branches can be treated in the same way. Wisterias are favorite plants for this treatment, but grape vines, European hornbeams and fruit trees also do very well.

SWAGS

Evidence from sculpture, paintings and mosaics found at Pompeii and Herculaneum suggests that the Romans found alluring the idea of twining the slender stems of climbing plants around ropes hanging in loose swags. Such a combination of art and nature is most appealing. It is certainly a delightful idea, which can be adapted as another means of screening different areas of the garden or providing visual limits to a vista.

Rope or chain hangs down in decorative curves from the tops of a row of columns. Plants are then encouraged to climb up the columns and along the swags. Ivy is particularly effective used in this way, especially if several swags are used between each pair of columns. The materials used can vary widely from wooden posts and stout rope to cut stone pillars and bronze chain; one of the most attractive swag screens I have seen was made of massive, ship's tow rope hung between heavy wooden pillars.

PLANTED PILLARS & OBELISKS

In most gardens, a strong vertical feature at some point adds to the interest of the composition and can have a screening or dividing role. A single pillar or an elegant obelisk half buried in greenery has a delightfully romantic effect.

In this situation, wood or masonry columns often provide the right, deliberately substantial air. Climbers will be encouraged if a thick cladding of galvanized wire mesh is wrapped round the base of the column. Climbing roses, clematis and, especially, honeysuckles look lovely when attached to single pillars in this way

In formal gardens, obelisks in cut stone can be very striking; romantic versions are usually made in a tracery of trelliswork or welded steel. In this

PLANTED PILLARS
Simple pillars can be made from tall fragments of formal masonry columns or just stout wooden posts and serve as excellent freestanding supports for climbers.

OBELISKS
Using rough cut rather than smooth planed lumber to construct obelisks helps them support climbing plants.

form they provide perfect support for climbing plants and make a softer outline than the strictly vertical single pillar. In either material, they were a popular feature in many Victorian gardens and they do add a charmingly old-fashioned air to the garden.

Trellis obelisks consist of four simple panels held together on strong supporting posts. Even in a small garden the apex of an obelisk should be at least 2.2m/7ft off the ground, to command attention. If more height and dignity are required, the obelisk can be set on top of a 50cm/18in high cube of stone or brick. This has the additional advantage of preventing contact with the soil which would encourage the wood to rot. Welded mild steel obelisks are constructed from panels in the same way but look slightly lighter and more airy. No matter what color is chosen for them, a thorough coating of an anticorrosive paint is essential.

THE PASSAGE
— THROUGH THE —
GARDEN

The passage through the romantic garden should be a journey of exploration, in an atmosphere of secrecy and mystery. The siting of the walkways will be determined largely by the placing of the screens, caverns and glades and, also, of the special features discussed in the next chapter. You should not have paths too straight or formal-looking, and should make them of attractive materials that in themselves provide a lure for the visitor. Where possible, their edges should always be overgrown, and they should blend in with the natural contours of the garden. Tracks on steeply sloping land should rise slowly across the contours, winding back on themselves like sheeptracks. If they are too wide or involve too much excavation they will be obtrusive, although some leveling may be necessary for comfortable going.

PATHS

Paths that are subject to frequent use or are used for transport will have to be hard surfaced. The choice of material is usually dictated by local geology, and it is wise to stick to local materials. Imports, however romantic they may look in their own location, never blend in entirely satisfactorily. Marble is therefore unlikely to be a choice for many of us, but old bricks and weathered stone make wonderful paths. Within a short time they look as if they have been laid for centuries, especially if some of the gaps between the individual elements are not pointed up, so that seedlings take root and soften the outline. In this case it is often best to allow nature a fairly

ABOVE This charming and informal old brick path is beautifully complemented by the pleasingly disordered mixed beds through which it meanders. Candelabra primulas, Welsh poppies, lilies, royal ferns and skunk cabbage are among the plants which jostle for place, engendering a feeling of luxuriance and offering a wonderful variety of foliage and flower forms and colors.

RIGHT Flintstones appropriate to the region have been used to make a lovely and original decorative paving to the approach and the walls of this charming hump-backed bridge. The arch was constructed in brick formed over a piece of curved corrugated iron which was removed when the mortar binding the bricks had set. It links two sections of a wonderfully romantic garden (shown on pp 96-101).

free hand – you can remove a few pernicious weeds – since artificially dotted plants on a path or terrace can be very obvious.

Bricks can be laid in a dozen different patterns, although always for preference on edge. Care should be taken to select frost-proof bricks that will not split and crumble if water penetrates and then freezes, although the romantic gardener will ignore modern engineering bricks. If old-stock or handmade bricks are not available, a very wide range of 'antique' bricks are now produced, and assume a patina of age more readily on the ground than when used in a wall.

'Crazy paving' is only appropriate where large irregular pieces of old stone are available. A more soothing effect is created by using rectangular slabs of weathered stone, if you can afford them. They are expensive both to buy and to lay, but provide the most aesthetically pleasing walking surface and background to plants in temperate gardens. Reconstituted stone or even concrete paving slabs can be made visually interesting if laid in conjunction with other materials. One example is to intersect slabs with lines of paving bricks or thin lumber strips. As a rule, use no more than two materials together, to avoid a cluttered effect. A brick edging to a flag path can also be very effective.

In gardens in warm climates, thick handmade terracotta tiles can be an effective substitute for stone, and could perhaps be used on a terrace to provide an exterior link with tiles laid inside the house or conservatory. In more northerly places, a lumber deck looks very attractive and appropriate. If you have access to a sawmill, you could consider using lumber blocks or disks for your narrower paths. Alternative small-scale materials are cobbles, laid in a choice of pattern, Belgian blocks, or paving bricks. Whatever type of material you select, do be sure that it is in keeping with the period of your house, especially if you have an historic house.

Very fine rock chippings or very coarse sands in gray or subdued red or ocher shades make a good general cover for pathways through romantic gardens. If the area involved is not too large, they can also be used to clothe the planted areas, suppressing weeds and avoiding the need for formal path edging to keep the loose fill in place. Once the topping has settled into the hard-packed core, the paths will seem as if they had simply been trodden smooth by the feet of generations of travelers. If drainage is a problem, strategically placed weathered stone slabs can be set into the grit, ensuring that the top lies flush with the general surface level. If large areas of this sort are necessary, they can be arranged to look like the foundations of ancient buildings rediscovered. Fed with cues like this, the imagination conjures up a feeling of trespassing through time.

These grits provide a relatively 'soft' dry pathway, defract light more attractively and look more romantic than many soils. They are often encountered naturally in woodland, where generations of heavy raindrops from the tree canopy have made the coarser particles in the soil rise to the surface. This simulated naturalness can also be provided by bark chippings. These are now available in various grades, whose size may be selected to be in scale with the area to be covered. Both bark chippings and grit may be spread over black plastic sheeting which, while utterly unromantic in itself, does have the advantage of suppressing weed growth and freeing the romantic gardener for further contemplation. On no account should the plastic ever be visible, or the illusion is shattered.

Moving onto a grit surface, especially from an area of hardstanding, induces a remarkably conspiratorial mood. Footfalls are muffled, allowing romantic sounds like birdsong and the rustling of leaves in the wind to become evident. The ability to move quietly also increases the feeling of secrecy which is an important element in the romantic garden.

Grass paths provide a marvelous contrast when stepping off, for example, a Tennessee fieldstone terrace, and will be fine if they are well drained and not subject to very heavy use. They also provide the gentlest of links between grass areas. While a smallish conventional mown lawn may be appropriate near the house, grassy areas – like the central glades in your leafy caverns – will need a more romantic covering, such as a wildflower or primula meadow, or a fragrant thyme or chamomile lawn. Unusual and lovely, purely decorative, alternatives to the lawn can also be produced by planting plain stands of ornamental grass. Three of these are particularly useful. *Holcus mollis* 'Variegatus' has a variegated gray-green and cream foliage and spreads quickly to form a bright sward if planted at 23cm/9in intervals. *Sisyrinchium angustifolium*, blue-eyed grass, is a tiny member of the Iris family with grasslike leaf blades, producing vivid blue flowers in early summer. It does spread, though rather slowly, and needs planting at 15cm/6in intervals. Planted at similar intervals *Festuca glauca* will soon fuse to form a sward which looks like a silvery blue haze.

STEPS

Linking different levels by means of steps can provide a vertical dynamic in the garden but must be handled with care when linking areas of different materials, such as terrace to path, for example. If you are moving from a rectangularly paved terrace – perhaps with some decrepit balustrading entwined with wisteria, deliberately looking like the relics of some former grand scheme now overtaken by rampant nature – then the steps should reflect this romantic character. Visual appeal and practicality must be balanced to a nicety: while the risers may be chipped, offering footholds for *Corydalis lutea* or *Campanula muralis* and the interstices of the paving blocks softened with tiny alpine pinks, it is best if the treads themselves are level and firm.

Both brick and stone can be used, sometimes combined, as seen in some of the elaborate confections of the Edwardian period. Steps in the garden should provide easy going while never being so shallow as to offer the possibility of tripping. Similar rules apply to less formal steps, which can be made by fitting stout wooden planks as risers, held on edge by thick steel rods driven into the ground, and then back-filled with earth and gravel. In a woodland setting, split logs could be used instead of sawn lumber. A coat of wire netting will prevent them becoming slippery in wet weather. While remaining effective as a tread, the mesh soon disappears beneath a layer of accumulated soil and leaf mold.

LEFT A simple mown grass pathway makes a perfect passage through informal parts of the garden. Nothing could be better here, where cowslips and naturalized narcissi dominate an enchanting wildflower meadow in spring. Note how by providing a contrast the mown pathway hints that it is an area which is cared for rather than being just a pretty wilderness.

BRIDGES

In a journey through the garden, there is something strangely attractive about being able to walk above water and peer into its depths. It is a little like the sensation of flying, and it must have something to do with the unusualness of the experience for normally earthbound creatures, embodying as it does the tremors of both fear and delight. Because it is suitably other-wordly, it is worth trying to include in any garden, and a bridge crossing the corner of a small pond or over a little streamlet can provide at least some of this excitement.

Effective, single span bridges over small water features can be as simple as two strong parallel beams of lumber, topped with strong wooden transverse planks and supported by a stone or concrete platform at each end. If the penalty for tumbling from the bridge is unlikely to be too severe, they don't even need any form of supporting handrail. But if one is considered necessary it can be suspended from posts set in the bridge support platforms. Really tiny rills or rivulets can often be bridged by simply laying a big slab of thick flat stone between both of the banks an inch or two above the water surface. Even standing on something as small as that will induce a pleasingly different sensation

Making very romantic wooden bridges – like that which features in Monet's paintings of his waterlily garden – which are frequently arched and have a rusticated look, requires craftsmanship of a high order but can be worth the expense because they are so very beautiful. However, even simple single-span bridges can be given much romantic appeal if, for example, they are used as the base of a pergola over which a wisteria or a clematis is encouraged to rampage.

LEFT Ancient-looking stone steps, overgrown and uneven, cannot fail to look romantic, however impractical they may be to use. Whenever possible, flights of steps, the route of paths or the course of streams should curve away out of sight behind screens of foliage or masonry. This always tempts a visitor to go forward to discover what lies beyond.

ATMOSPHERIC EFFECTS

The creation and maintenance of a romantic atmosphere within the garden can be achieved by subtle effects and careful touches. It goes without saying that nothing too new is ever likely to look romantic. New wood for structures should be stained to banish its newness immediately. Dull browns or very dark matt greens are good colors, but sometimes some of the blue stains can be very attractive. Provided it is sound, old wood should be used whenever possible. Planks which have been weathered for years and in which the grain has become exposed in relief look marvelous.

If new stone or brick has to be utilized, it should be painted with yogurt, or a slurry of cow manure in water, to stain it temporarily and encourage the growth of mosses and lichens to hasten the aging process and create the look of antiquity. On no account should brightly colored modern plastic furniture or such items as modern mechanical barbecues be allowed to destroy the atmosphere in the garden. As well as the use of unobtrusively dark-colored materials, the careful contrast of light and dark effects –

BRIDGES
Standing above flowing water is always a romantic experience. In a small garden it can be provided very simply by a large rock spanning a streamlet. Over larger expanses of water a wide arched base can be decorated with a wooden pergola, planted with climbers.

A simple wooden bridge can look especially inviting if the planks run in the direction of the crossing. They should be screwed to a strong stable box frame, whose bottom longitudinal member can be cut in a curve to give the bridge an attractive shape when seen from the side.

MOONLIGHT
Attractive features such as statues should be situated in places where they can be lit, at least partially, by moonlight on clear nights.

CANDLELIGHT
On dark nights a single candle can lighten quite a large area of a garden with the enchanting movement of its soft flickering light.

CONTRAST
Just as interesting contrasts of plant color and shape are important, contrasting light and shady areas should be provided by the garden as a whole. Thick, dark copses of taller shrubs and trees should, for example, surround sunny glades.

both by day and by night – can be specially atmospheric, as can the deliberate evocation of, for example, exotic sunny climes in cooler and more somber climates.

LIGHT & DARK

Drama can be created and the atmosphere heightened by contrasts in plant color, and the magic of the garden can be enhanced by creating contrasts of light and shade during the journey around the garden. A dark foreground planting of, say, evergreen viburnums and hollies should be pierced to allow a view of a bright central area, perhaps the pale colors of an early summer border, with the first roses and delphiniums, campanulas and iris. Similarly, a pale lichened

statue will stand out against its background of ancient yew, while the pale colors of a border recede yet remain clear against a perimeter planting of conifers.

Light and dark effects are heightened at night. Even mundane gardens are highly romantic by moonlight on a balmy summer's evening. Fragrance lingers on the air, pale colors have an intensity they lack during the day, and the wonderful silvery quality of the light transfigures the outstanding features, leaving the garden's defects lost in profound shadow.

On warm yet moonless nights the romantic gardener's frustration can be alleviated by the use of garden lighting. The intention is not to present the garden as if it were a floodlit tennis court, but rather to enhance certain features, to attract attention deeper into the garden, to maintain the magic and the mystery. If you intend to do more than set up the simplest system, calling in specialist help is essential – electricity is as dangerous in the garden as elsewhere, unless properly harnessed. The mechanical aspects should obviously be concealed as far as possible: armored cable should be buried at least 50cm/18in deep, possibly alongside a path for easy retrieval, and the individual units should be placed inconspicuously so that you are neither offended by their housing during the day nor dazzled by misplaced glare at night.

Do remember as a principle that it is almost impossible to underlight. Only low wattage bulbs will be needed and it is better by far to spotlight just one feature – perhaps the inside canopy of one particular tree. High-pressure sodium lights will give a warmer impression than the rather blue light given off by mercury lights. Lights can be moved around, too, especially if specialist help has been sought to give you a safe and flexible system. Sometimes flooding a nondescript area with a diffused low-level green glow can be dramatic, although generally subtlety will produce the most roman-

tic effects. Outdoor candles, although providing a very dim glow, can be carefully sited to help display intriguing plant forms in silhouette. Because they flicker in the breeze, they can also provide enchanting shadow-play effects.

EXOTIC ROMANCE

Nostalgia for happy, sunnier times and vacations passed in beautiful places is a poignant emotion. which can be provoked by the designs of certain areas of even the darkest romantic garden. Artefacts such as large fragments of amphorae collected from Aegean beaches or vast earthenware jars gingerly transported from Spain or Mexico can be incorporated. Special areas like sunny terraces should be set aside and planted with exotics, such as Chusan palms or conservatory-grown bougainvillea or frangipani put out in tubs for the summer. You could provide an area in which all the fragrant Mediterranean herbs can be grown, in full sun, releasing their fragrances and with them memories of notable vacation times. Such areas might prompt musings about the more innocent-seeming early world, which produced stories like the romance of Daphnis and Chloe and acted as the cradle of our western civilization; stimuli which are perfectly in accord with the ideals of the romantic movement.

WARM MEMORIES
A terrace that catches the sun can be set out with earthenware amphorae, vases of tumbling geraniums, plants with exotic spiky foliage and surfaced with terracotta tiles. Even in cold climates, such a spot, in summer, can evoke memories of warmer places and happy times.

A MOATED GARDEN

Small, romantic garden 'rooms' have been created within this larger garden, whose furniture includes a romantic arbor, created by growing two 'Constance Spry' climbing roses over a simple frame above and around a stone bench. Roses (right) cascade down toward richly planted herbaceous borders in the central grass alley. Together with a pair of sentinel conifers, they make a perfect frame for the classical bust that terminates the vista.

A moated castle site, with one of the original towers still standing and forming part of a more recent manor house, could be regarded as somewhat forbidding. That is clearly what the owners wanted to avoid when they resolved to design this garden to exploit all the romantic qualities latent in the ancient masonry and calm, reflective water. As the garden now stands, the masonry acts as a wonderful foil for an astonishing, year-round pageant of flowering plants.

The house itself is on a rectangular island surrounded by an area of garden, connected by a splendid, robust, wooden bridge to a second, and larger, island devoted entirely to gardens. Although both island gardens have been formally laid out, any rigidity that might have ensued has been banished by the glory of the planting. The effect when walking in these gardens is of being immersed in a jungle of foliage and flower with all sense of layout completely obscured.

On the practical side, large areas close to the house have been paved to give dry standing and a convenient place for outdoor dining in summer. The regularity of the paving is echoed in a canal-side line of dwarf spruce – *Picea glauca* 'Albertiana Conica' – which grow only slowly and do not need shearing to maintain their neat, conical shape.

One large and three smaller rectangular beds (two with formal, low box hedges) further divide the terrace, while the area in front of the tower has its own pattern-paved court enclosed on two sides by high hedges, through which visitors must stroll to reach the bridge to the second garden.

The profusion of the planting in the large, mixed bed and of the climbers, notably roses and clematis, is by far the most dominant feature here. Its impact is reinforced by a shallow border of herbaceous plants, including white geraniums, blue campanulas and alliums, with some apple-pink-blossomed escallonia bushes to provide vertical height and interest.

Moving across the bridge, the visitor finds four small rectangles formed by grass alleys lined

with tall hedges. At the junction of the alleys, the hedges have been planted further apart to form a circular area with, at its center, a raised stone urn and sentinel, columnar conifers stationed in each of the four quadrants.

Each of the small gardens has its own distinctive character. One of them is so densely planted with perennials that a large cluster of mixed delphiniums, which ought to resemble skyscrapers on a city skyline, appear no more outstanding than a freckle of daisies on a lawn. In wonderful contrast, the neighboring garden is a simple green basilica with a plain marginal seat and a short central stone column sitting on a green carpet of lawn; a place of total repose after the delirium of the previous floral fantasy.

ABOVE The graceful forms of the roses violet 'Veilchenblau' and pink 'Francois Juranville' use the sturdy, wooden bridge joining the house to the garden across the moat as a climbing frame.

RIGHT Viewed along the moat, the effectiveness of the high perimeter trees in enclosing the garden and acting as a dark, contrasting backdrop for the roses on the bridge can be fully appreciated.

While flowering shrubs dominate the third rectangle, in the fourth it is roses, which also predominate in all the planted areas and are a major contributor to the overwhelming romantic quality of the whole garden.

The owners chose each rose of the hundreds planted for its vigor and traditional appearance. Even the relatively modern shrub rose 'Constance Spry' has the look and fragrance of a nineteenth-century cabbage rose. The repeat-flowering, fragrant 'Pink Cloud' is another post-war rose judged sufficiently worthy of inclusion. But it is the great classical roses of the last century, such as the cerise-flowered Bourbon climber 'Zephirine Drouhin', which have pride of place in the garden, where a section has been devoted to each type.

ALPHABETICAL PLANT LIST
Abelia × *grandiflora*
Akebia quinata
Alchemilla mollis
Allium aflatunense
Anemone japonica
A. nemorosa
Artemesia absinthium
'Lambrook Silver'
Arum italicum 'Marmoratum'
Bergenia 'Silberlicht'
Buxus sempervirens
Campanula burghalti
C. lactiflora
Carpinus betulus
Ceanothus 'Gloire de Versailles'
Choisya ternata
Chrysanthemum corymbosum
C. serotinum
Clematis alpina
C. fargesii
C. macropetala 'Rubra'

C. texensis 'Etoile Rose'
C. viticella 'Alba Luxurians'
C. 'Comtesse de Bouchaud'
C. 'Mme. Julia Correvon'
C. 'Perle d'Azur'
C. 'Yellow Queen'
Cornus florida
C. kousa
Corylopsis spicata
Corylus avellana
Crocus chrysanthus
Dephinium 'Blue Triomphator'
D. 'F. W. Smith'
D. 'Finsteraarhorn'
Dicentra spectabilis
Enkianthus campanulatus
Eranthus hyemalis
Escallonia 'Donard Seedling'
Euonymus alatus
Euphorbia palustris
E. wulfenii
Fritillaria imperialis
Fuchsia magellanica
Galanthus nivalis

Geranium endressii
G. macrorrhizum
G. m. 'Album'
G. pratense
Geum rivale
Ginkgo biloba
Gleditsia triacanthos
Hamamelis intermedia
'Ruby Glow'
H. mollis
Helleborus foetidus
H. niger
H. orientalis
Hosta fortunei
'Aureomarginata'
H. sieboldiana
Hydrangea arborescens
H. macrophylla
H. paniculata 'Grandiflora'
H. petiolaris
Iris foetidissima
I. unguicularis
Jasminum officinale
Juniperus communis 'Suecica'

Leucojum vernum
Lysimachia punctata
Magnolia × soulangeana
Malus floribunda
M. 'John Downie'
Meconopsis betonicifolia
Nothofagus antarctica
Paeonia lutea 'Ludlowii'
P. suffruticosa
Parthenocissus tricuspidata
Petasites fragrans
Phlox paniculata 'Lavendelwolke'
Picea glauca 'Albertiana Conica'
Pieris 'Forest Flame'
Polygonum campanulatum
P. macrophyllum
Populus nigra
Primula auricula
P. florindae
P. veris
Prunus cerasifera 'Atropurpurea'
P. serrulata 'Amanogawa'
P. subhirtella 'Autumnalis'
Pyrus salicifolia
Rhododendron lutescens
R. micranthum
Rosa ×alba 'Semi-plena'
R. californica 'Plena'
R. centifolia 'Muscosa'
R. 'Constance Spry'
R. damascena
R. × dupontii
R. eglanteria
R. filipes 'Kiftsgate'
R. 'Francois Juranville'
R. gallica
R. g. 'Officinalis'
R. g. 'Versicolor'
R. moschata
R. multiflora
R. muscosa
R. 'Pink Cloud'
R. rubiginosa
R. spinosissima
R. 'Veilchenblau'
R. willmottiae
R. 'Zephirine Drouhin'
Ruta graveolens
Salvia pratensis
Sarcococca humilis
Saxifraga cortusifolia
Scabiosa columbaria
Solanum jasminoides
Sorbus vilmorinii
Syringa microphylla 'Superba'
Tamarix tetandra
Taxus baccata
Tulipa sylvestris
Ulmus minor 'Wredei'
Viburnum × bodnantense
V. plicatum 'Mariesii'
V. tinus
Vinca minor
Viola cornuta

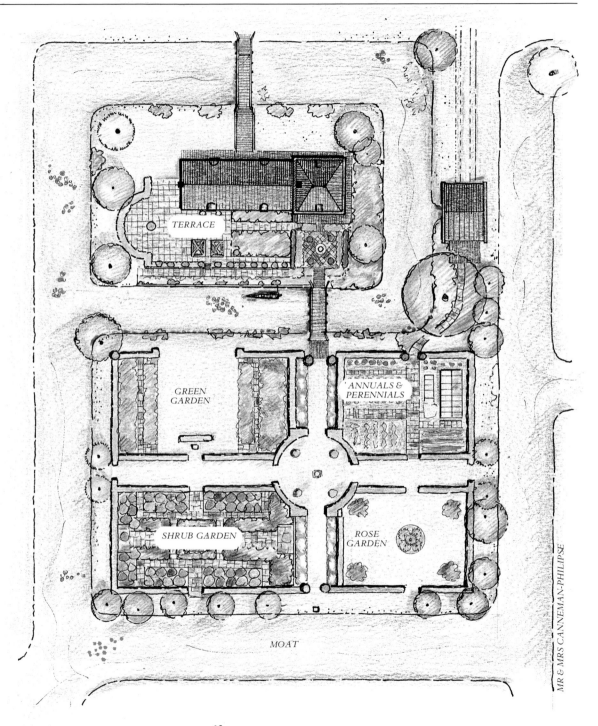

TERRACE

GREEN
GARDEN

ANNUALS &
PERENNIALS

SHRUB GARDEN

ROSE
GARDEN

MOAT

MR & MRS CANNEMAN-PHILIPSE

A SECLUDED GARDEN

This superbly designed garden is, in effect, a series of glades surrounded by leafy caverns, here formed by ancient trees and reinforced by heavy marginal planting. Note the effectiveness of a color scheme in which a predominantly dark green background has been highlighted with a silver, paler green to bring variety and interest. A simple, white seat (right) takes the eye deep into the heart of the garden. Although the designer has used quite a formal planting plan, the choice and positioning of plants produce a truly mysterious and romantic garden environment.

The site of this city garden is typical of those found not far from the central areas of many large conurbations. There are still trees in these areas, relics from former farming days, worth preserving, and others were planted along garden boundaries when the land was split up and built on. The result is that these properties tend to be well screened from their neighbors by a mature backdrop of fine foliage, and so at least one of the romantic gardener's major tasks – that of providing an atmosphere of seclusion and privacy – has already been accomplished.

In this garden, the main change has been the planting of shrubs, trees and herbaceous plants in large mixed beds, which project from the margins toward the center of the lawn, destroying any impression of a rectangular plot. Now, there is a series of leafy caverns with open lawn glades at their heart. None of them can be fully appreciated, however, until it is penetrated and its secrets revealed. It is an interesting feature here that the romantic atmosphere is not dependent on the introduction of garden structures.

Adjoining the house is a seating terrace partially screened from the lawn area by a loose hedge of roses, featuring a simple, rustic pole archway supporting yet more roses. A painted wooden seat has been provided both for convenience and to attract the eye into one of the secret places further down the garden. Elsewhere, the light, natural color of an attractive stone bust of a Renaissance woman invites speculation about a very dark cavern beyond, and a large, dark vase adds vertical interest to a lawn glade.

But the real magic and romance of this garden is due to a great extent to the magnificent selection of plants and the informal and very thoughtful, way they have been planted within a carefully structured, almost formal, design. All the characteristics of form, shape and color have been exploited: tall, spiky and erect ornamental thistles, such as *Onopordum*, are stationed to mark the entrances to caverns, but a clear vista through the gap is denied by the lax fronds and mistily silver foliage of two weeping pears.

Purple-leaved salvias, towering, stately foxgloves, gauzy cotton lavender and full-skirted ladies mantle crowd the feet of burgeoning old roses, creating color and variety at all levels.

Cleverly, the garden initially offers only inviting glimpses of its half-hidden charms.

Ivies and clematis have been encouraged to climb high on the trunks and into the crowns of some of the taller trees. And instead of completely removing the remains of a huge, old tree that lost its head in a storm, 6m/20ft of its bare trunk have been retained as an outsized climbing post for a Russian vine, *Polygonum baldschuanicum*, which has turned it into an amazing, green totem pole competing strongly for attention when clad in its flaky white flower chains.

As a general background for the flower color, shrubs and perennials with darker green foliage

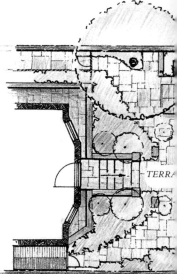

TERRA

ARABELLA LENNOX-BOYD

have been chosen. But to avoid any hint of drabness, the mixture has been discreetly laced with areas of gray, silver and brighter, more acidic greens with, very occasionally, a few small dashes of a more passionate dark red. With a few exceptions – where something more outstanding, such as a lemon yellow, has been demanded by the design – the plants chosen are the paler shades of blue, and pink or the most transparent of whites.

Quite understandably, the designer believes that roses – particularly the fragrant, old roses, the species roses and many of the early climbers and ramblers – are the plants most likely to engender a romantic atmosphere, and the garden is packed with them. Pruned only to eliminate any ugly, old wood or to encourage additional flowering, they have rampaged everywhere in the garden, with single shrubs evolving into plant copses with high, arching margins and climbers almost threatening to scale and smother everything within reach.

In summer, the effect is of one tremendous, perception-baffling, floral crescendo.

PLANT LIST

TERRACE
Aesculus hippocastianum
Viburnum tinus
Crambe cordifolia
Paeonia lutea
Choysia ternata
Rosa 'Canary Bird'
Lavandula spica
Buxus sempervirens
Clematis montana
Ceanothus 'Cascade'
Wisteria sinensis
Rosa 'Fantin Latour'
Alchemilla mollis

1ST GLADE
Pyrus communis
Magnolia × soulangeana
Viburnum opulus
Pyracantha rogersiana
Viburnum burkwoodii
Lonicera serotina and *L. belgica* trained as standards
Roses including 'Fritz Nobis', 'Dreaming spires', 'Mme Isaac Perriere', 'Iceberg', Nozomi', 'Queen of Denmark'
Helichrysum angustifolium
Agapanthus umbellatus
Geranium spp.

2ND GLADE
Pyrus salicifolia 'Pendula'
Viburnum plicatum 'Mariesii'
Syringa persica and *S.* 'Blue Hyacinth'
Forsythia suspensa
Polygonum baldschuanicum
Cercis siliquastrum 'Album'
Taxus baccata (as hedging)
Cupressus spp.
Senecio grey
Osmanthus delavayi
Stachys 'Silver carpet'
Hosta glauca
Buddleia alternifolia
Roses including *R. spinosissima, R. rubrifolia, R. gallica,* 'Mme Louis Laperriere', 'Buff Beauty', 'Nevada', 'Paul's Lemon Pillar', 'Cecile Brunner', 'New Dawn', 'Iceberg'

3RD GLADE
Pyrus communis
Syringa spp.
Prunus subhirtella 'Autumnalis'
Philadelphus virginale
Aucuba japonica
Laburnum voisii
Ribes album
Acer pseudoplatanus
Tilia euchlora
Hydrangea petiolaris

Crataegus spp.
Azaleas including 'Christopher Wren', 'Mollis', 'Toucan',
Rosa 'Zephirine Drouhin'

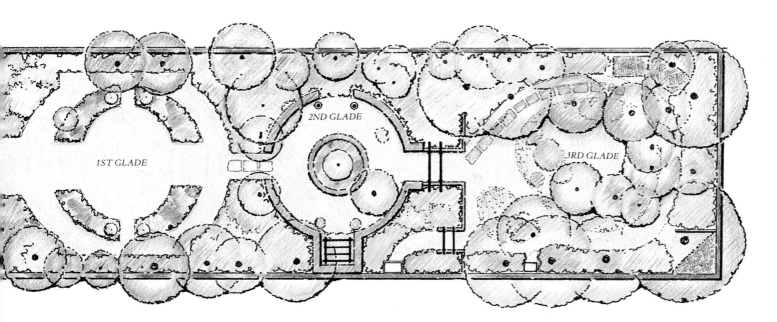

THE SECRETS OF THE GARDEN

nce you have created the secluded sanctuary, and enticed the visitor to wander deep into the garden with the promise of romance within, you must reveal the secrets of the garden. To be truly satisfying the romantic garden should provide treasures to reward explorers. These can be as simple and satisfying as a superbly grown and fascinating plant, or an arbor which invites quiet repose, or an intriguing pot or statue. These features must maintain their promise when examined close at hand, and, ideally, should impart to their surroundings an atmosphere of antiquity, fantasy, drama or surprise.

PLACES FOR QUIET REFLECTION

Once established, good romantic gardens should be places for light garden' fidgeting, rather than vigorous gardening exercise. The errant stem of a climber might need gently coaxing back into place here, the fading bloom of a rose removing there; but there should be nothing too pressing or burdensome, leaving plenty of time simply to daydream or to think. So, suitably cloistered corners have to be created for this therapeutic reverie. They can consist of something as basic as a bench seat or as sophisticated as a tranquil arcade, but to minimize the risk of interruption, these areas of repose should be located as far away from the house as possible, or at least hidden from it.

SEATS

Some of the coziest seats can be easily created as a niche in the masonry of a wall as it is being made. The higher the back, the more secluded the seat seems, because solid masonry cuts out sound more effectively than any other material. A disadvantage of the stone or brick seat is the length of time it takes to dry out thoroughly after rain, but this can be overcome by topping it with a dark-stained wooden deck which will dry out much more quickly. Even less formal dry-weather seating can be provided by simply mounting a smooth heavy wooden plank such as a railroad tie on stone building blocks or brick plinths set against a wall.

Elegant, freestanding seats can be made by craftsmen, either to a personal design or reproducing the more romantic eighteenth-century models. These will justify their expense, if chosen with sufficient care, by greatly increasing the lyrical quality of the garden. However, a real search can yield less costly and simpler, but nevertheless attractive, designs. These are usually genuine or reproduction Victorian seats, in which a curved iron framework supports either broad wooden planking or narrow wooden laths. If you can find an old one, even in poor condition, it can usually be repaired. Unless it is too badly corroded, broken iron can be repaired or reinforced by welding, and wood is easy to replace. Because their iron framework gives them a softer-looking form, these old Victorian seats, and good reproductions of them, are infinitely preferable to their more utilitarian modern counterparts.

A perfectly contrived romantic garden feature has been made by turning the inside of a corner of a ruined building into an enchanting secular sanctuary. Bricking up the old doorway and flanking it with noble columns set on semilunar steps has given it the dignity of a shrine. It makes a fine setting for an elegant figure whose attributes are rather thought-provoking – the garb and coiffure are those of a gentleman, but the spade is the implement of a humble tiller of the soil.
The idyllic nature of the corner, with tumbling creeper festooning the walls and a light foreground curtain of maple foliage is enchanting. Leaf debris and moss growing on the masonry add to its charm, while a large mirror behind the figure plays tricks with the perceptions, enabling it to be examined in two views simultaneously.

LEFT The highly fragrant Clematis armandii *is wonderfully placed to sweeten the air about a seat whose solid stone and elegant shape has a romantic grandeur.*

BELOW A climbing rose entwined with ivy climbing over an arched frame makes the perfect arbor to house this fine Victorian cast-iron seat. Its elaborate tracery marries well with the formality of the paving.

Less comfortable, but attractive and quite suitable for a short pause in a meander round the garden, is the stone bench. Simple benches consist of a slab of masonry mounted on decorative stone plinths, some of which are simply scrolled and fluted, while others are sculpted to represent heraldic animals. The more elaborate stone seats, complete with stone backs and arms, can look wonderfully romantic when moss and lichens have begun to develop on their surfaces, but their scale is too grand for most gardens.

No matter what sort of seat is chosen, it is essential to position it so that it offers its occupant the pleasure of an interesting view. Unless the view behind the seat is particularly splendid, the setting of the seat should not be too open. A freestanding seat can be made to seem more hospitable if a hedge or line of shrubs is planted behind it and along its sides. Evergreens, such as yew, *Taxus × media,* and the common (or cherry) laurel *Prunus laurocerasus,* would make a good choice. Alternatively, you can build a 1.5m/5ft high, partially enclosing wall to back the seat. And there are few more romantic places to locate a seat than a secluded arbor.

ARBORS

It isn't difficult to reinforce the sense of mystery invoked in a romantic garden by making some kind of arbor where people can sit unseen and enjoy its atmosphere. It was a pleasure clearly enjoyed by John Dryden, who, in describing a fine one said:

'Both roof and sides were like a Parlour made,
A soft Recess, and a cool Summer Shade,
The Hedge was set so thick, no Foreign Eye
The Persons plac'd within it could espy'.

We clearly understand Dryden's pleasure because good arbors, which should almost totally surround seats, reinforce the idea that a romantic garden is a leafy haven that totally excludes the outside world. This atmosphere of comforting safety and privacy is why in literature, and clearly also in life, arbors have so frequently been the setting for declarations of love.

There are various relatively simple ways of making an arbor. Often something as ordinary as an old and shabby wooden garden shed can be upgraded by cutting away its side, replacing it with two strong and simple wooden columns to support the roof, and smothering the whole structure in attractive creepers: the Virginia creepers for cover and autumn color, ivies for year-round privacy, and *Jasminum officinale* for flower and scent in milder areas.

A tall, thick, hedge growing inside a wall or fence, can provide a ready-made site for an

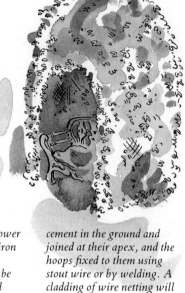

A SECLUDED HEDGE
Removing a few plants in an existing hedge, pruning the newly exposed edges and planting climbers to scramble up posts placed on either side of the gap is a quick way of making a pretty arbor.

A GREEN HELMET
A freestanding leafy bower can be made round an iron frame. Concrete reinforcement rods can be bent to form arches and hoops, arranged as shown. The arches should be set in

cement in the ground and joined at their apex, and the hoops fixed to them using stout wire or by welding. A cladding of wire netting will support a host of climbers planted round the edge.

A WOODEN RETREAT
With a little imagination, ugly buildings can be made to look more romantic. Removing the side from a garden shed and replacing it with strong wooden pillars and then covering the structure with climbing plants can turn it into an attractive arbor.

arbor. First, prune back some of the shrubs or trees composing the hedge to make room for a seat set back against the wall. Initially the portion of hedge flanking the seat will be rather barren, but this will soon 'green up' as the plants obtain more access to light. A pair of upright wooden posts stationed at the garden-facing corners of the hedge gap can be used to support climbing plants such as honeysuckle and clematis; trained along a strong wire or thick rope joining the top of the posts, these will soon form a high leafy arch which will increase the feeling of intimacy in the sitting area. When the climbers are growing well, you can then lead some stems back to the wall to form a partial foliage roof.

If you have a fence or wall but no hedge, you can use trellis to provide an attractive frame for plants. Flank the seat with two open-topped trellis-sided 'pillars' or 'boxes', supported by strong posts and set against a wall, which in turn act as supports for a simple pergola-type roof.

Two columnar Irish yews, *Taxus baccata* 'Fastigiata', planted inside each trellis box will eventually form a solid barrier of evergreen foliage. English ivy, *Hedera helix*, planted along the outside of the trellis boxes will quickly cover the flanks and scramble over the pergola structure to make a complete canopy of leaf. As the yew grows, whenever its shoots project from the trellis frame they can be pruned away to encourage the plants to thicken and fill the box. The panels of trellis facing into the garden can be used to support flowering climbers like wisterias, climbing roses or clematis.

One of the quickest ways of making a leafy arbor is to make a giant green crusader's helmet out of a structure made from three metal arches set into the ground and joined at their apex.

Cover the whole structure, except space left for the entrance, with soft wire netting. Plant the perimeter with English ivy or, in colder climates, Virginia creeper. Soon these will smother it

A TRELLIS ARBOR
Two trellis-sided 'boxes' set against a wall either side of a seat can make an intimate arbor. Supported by strong posts held in metal post holders, the boxes should be about 53cm/21in wide, 91cm/36in deep and 2m/6 1/2ft high and in turn support a simple wood-frame roof. Hedge plants inside the boxes will ultimately become green walls, and climbers planted outside will cover the whole structure with leaf.

GARLANDED SWINGS
A garlanded swing can be made by constructing a planter from strong, preservative-treated wood or galvanized anticorrosion-painted sheet metal. It should be suspended by strong steel straps and chain from either a sound strong tree branch or a purpose-built frame. A wooden seat can be fitted to the top of the planter between the chains, and the open-topped ends used to plant climbers. The planter must have drainage holes and be filled with moist peaty potting mix.

completely. It will make a perfect housing for a semicircular stone bench which, on a hot and sunny day, can provide enviable repose in a wonderful, cool green, subdued light.

GARLANDED SWINGS

Garlanded swings, supporting satin-clad and beribboned ladies, feature in some of the more lighthearted of eighteenth-century romantic paintings. Usually set in an enchanting glade, with all the characters improbably well groomed as though for a court function, these scenes must represent the wistful longings for a contemporary *dolce vita*. But no matter how revealing they may be about the spirit of that age, these paintings offer scant information about the construction of the swings themselves. Perhaps they represent the relics of some simply con-

RIGHT *In a hot and humid climate a simple gazebo of this kind, apart from offering an interesting view, can be quite a simple structure since it is only called upon to provide shade from the sun. This one makes a fine feature in a heavily wooded site and has open sides to admit cooling breezes.*

FAR RIGHT *This hexagonal trelliswork pavilion, with its slightly moghul appearance, makes a beautiful lure from afar. It is backed by a thick hedge and will provide an intimate haven from either sun or showers.*

structed apparatus of a woodman's childhood which, since being abandoned, has provided support for vines climbing up from the forest floor. It is difficult to tell. The detail is always lost behind the folds of a voluminous skirt. However that need not prevent ambitious romantic gardeners from having such a delightful feature in their garden.

A strong, swinging plant trough, attached by chains to a sturdy tree bough or purpose-built lumber arch can be made quite straightforwardly. You can plant it with three or four climbers such as ivy, honeysuckle or clematis – attaching them to the support chains as they grow – and a few shallow-rooted plants such as trailing lobelia, *Lobelia erinus,* and sweet violets, *Viola odorata,* to decorate the base. When fitted with a wooden seat (which can be removed to enable thorough watering and feeding) it will make a pretty seat for gentle rocking back and forth. Although it

will be too heavy to be used for vigorous swinging, and it will be essential to try and persuade children to use the chains and not the climbers as hand holds, such a garlanded swing will be a delight to sit on. Moreover, it will make a much more pleasing aesthetic contribution to the garden than any swinging seat bought at a garden center.

A lighter garlanded swing can be made by simply extending the lateral margins of a swing seat out beyond the suspension points of its supporting chains. These wings can have holes cut in them to take small pots, which can carry sufficient potting mix to support climbers like honeysuckle or one of the annual climbing nasturtiums, *Tropaeolum majus*. However, as the roots of the plants fill their small pots and their foliage increases, they will have very little reserve of water, and need watering at least once and perhaps twice a day in hot weather. And they will need feeding very frequently unless a genuine slow release fertilizer is added to the potting mix at the outset.

PAVILIONS

Since, for most of our lives, when we sit in shelter from wind and rain we are indoors in our houses or locked to our desks in offices, experiencing similar protection in a building deep in the garden induces a strange and delightfully liberating sense of truancy. And if being lost in Elysium is one of the exciting sensations a good romantic garden can provoke, finding a charming haven in which to rest in comfort is equally rewarding. Hence, buildings designed to offer more comfortable seating should be sited to be discovered on a walk or hidden from the house rather than being too obvious from it.

Once built, they are unlikely to be frequently used, so you can't hope to enjoy them alone; they will become the home of a myriad of creatures during your long absences – 'one of those sweet retreats which humane men erect for spiders' as Charles Dickens observed. While they might make some people nervous, no one can remain

SUMMER HOUSES

A simple framed hexagonal structure can make a fine summer house. It will seem light and airy, as well as pleasantly enclosed, if trelliswork, supporting a few climbing plants, covers its glass or open walls.

blind to spiders' amazing industry. Together with martins making mud nests under the eaves, flies which insist on coming in and then eternally buzzing to be let out, or the swarms of wasps which you will inevitably discover have been nesting there as soon as you open the apricot jelly, they will all extend the garden experience in a dynamic way. Meanwhile the building itself will soon begin to exude slightly mesmeric odors. Lumber, which has been soused in rain or absorbed winter dampness into the grain to be later cooked by the sun, will permeate the air with a mixed fragrance of mustiness, sparked up with a hint of resin. They will even help the garden to smell like Eden.

Pavilions are usually larger and more solid structures than arbors and while they may be well garnished with plants, their form is usually sufficiently satisfying and ambitious to look well without them. Their function allows them to be divided into two distinct types – the gazebos, or look-out posts, designed for the appreciation of a particular view, and summer houses, which ought to be sufficiently roomy to allow several people to be seated in comfort.

Gazebos are usually small buildings on a raised site, housing a seat offering spectacular views, hence they are most appropriate for large gardens. However, a different view of a familiar scene can add romance to any garden, and even a slight change in level can alter the whole perspective of a scene. If no suitable mount exists in the garden, and provided access to the site is at all reasonable, raising an earth mound on which a gazebo could be sited is very easy with the mechanical equipment available today.

Since they are in no sense residential, the building need not be very complicated. Gazebos must simply be robust enough to support a roof structure and remain standing no matter how strong the wind. It is best if they have a hard floor and deep foundations. But beyond that they can be anything, from a structure like a tiny loggia (see below) with seating for two, to a much larger hexagonal or octagonal construction with a complex roof form. What matters most to the romantic garden designer is that it is pretty and well scaled.

Summer houses are, notionally, shrines of bone china cups and wafer-thin cucumber sandwiches. But because they are enclosed structures capable of being made watertight, most summer houses end up as lamentable junk stores instead of being places to enjoy polite tea in the heart of the garden. Really pleasing factory-made summer houses are rare, and unless you find something ideal it may be better to build or have one built either to your own design or as an imitation of an eighteenth- or nineteenth-century model. A simple roofed hexagonal structure is a good framework to start with. Five of the sides can be given walls of glass or plexiglass set in a wooden frame and covered with trelliswork and – provided it isn't intended to become a home for junk or a serious toolshed – the sixth side can be left open.

LOGGIAS

Choice settings for *la dolce vita,* loggias can be among the most attractive of all garden features because they offer such an enchanted feeling of being suspended in a leafy limbo, half in and half out of doors. It is easy to understand why so many of the late nineteenth-century academic painters chose them as backgrounds for works in which ladies, dressed and coiffed like Roman matrons, grasp grapes from bunches hanging from a vine trained beneath a pergola roof, while their wistful hat-in-hand lovers eye bowls of fruit and silver detailed crystal wine decanters set like still lifes on woven cane tables.

Lovely loggias making fine places to sit and embodying a sense of seclusion can be made quite simply by suspending a pergola superstructure from a wall on one side and a line of columns on the other. It is a design that is capable of being greatly sophisticated. You can reduce drafts by 'walling' each end of the loggia with masonry or even plate glass, and this will make it useful for much longer on bright but breezy evenings. The sense of isolation can be increased by ensuring that the superstructure of the pergola is heavily clad with climbing plants or by making a tiled roof instead of an open pergola. You can use simple but attractive split-cane roller blinds to cut out excessive sunlight from the open sides of a loggia and this will also add to the sense of seclusion.

As long as you have a suitable wall, you can fit a loggia into quite a small garden, but to feel really comfortable a loggia needs to be slightly wider and higher than the average pergola, and it needs a hard floor. Patterns of tiles are attractive, but before the tiles are chosen it is vital to ensure that they are frost proof, as the loggia is, after all, outdoors.

ARCADES

Since the monastery cloister resulted from a deliberate choice of isolation from everyday affairs and a dedication to the spiritual, contemplative life, its secular counterpart, the arcade, carries with it a similar resonance. It is hard to walk alone in an arcade on a still and warm afternoon without seeming to hear the gentle shuffling of a monk's sandals or the distant but compelling chime of a bell calling him to Vespers. And that is an effect worth striving for by including an arcade in any romantic garden large enough to accommodate it.

Arcades are usually shallower and longer than loggias and always have a roof – usually sloping – unless they are inset into the side of a building. Among their advantages are that they provide somewhere shady to stroll at midday in the summer and also somewhere dry to take exercise

ROOFING
Old clay tiles, tiles of weathered slate or curved terracotta tiles are good roofing materials for loggias and arcades, giving them an air of permanence.

FLOORING
Well-laid decorative glazed tiles can give a pleasing indoor feeling in what is a protected outdoor situation.

ARCADES
An arcade is a more substantial structure than a loggia, and is for walking as well as sitting. It is perhaps best situated along a boundary wall, away from the distractions of the house. Soothing sounds can be provided by water trickling along a wall-mounted channel into a cistern, hidden below the floor. A submersible return-flow pump will circulate the water to a simple spout that feeds the channel.

LOGGIAS
Loggias need the backing of the house or a solid wall to feel suitably protected. However, in good weather they must provide the impression, for people using them, that they are in the garden and not the house, and so their structure should not look too solid. They can be constructed very simply from wooden columns and rafters, and the 'roof' can consist merely of creepers or vines, although a tiled roof provides better shelter.

DRAMATIC EFFECTS

when it rains. Arcades can be made along any wall that is approximately 2.5m/8ft high by supporting the inside of the roof frame against the wall and providing a line of columns to support its outer edge. To be really useful and comfortable for strolling, arcades should have a solid floor and be at least 12m/40ft long. They are therefore a feature more appropriate to the larger garden. However, set along one boundary wall, an arcade can provide wonderful isolation from the outside world, if space is available for such a feature.

Simple slates or terracotta Roman tiles make attractive roofing for an arcade. And the experience of strolling in one can be enhanced if a narrow, waist-high channel is built along the wall, conveying a trickle of water from a simple spout along its length. A few ferns in pots can be sat in the channel, and they will luxuriate in the damp and shady conditions.

Makers of romantic gardens can also be seen as embarking upon the creation of an escapist world of fantasy. This, too, is the domain of the theatre which, for a while, strives to suspend our disbelief, and ambitious romantic gardeners can play many theatrical tricks and try to produce dramatic effects.

Of course, much can be done to create a generally romantic atmosphere, as I have previously suggested, by the careful selection and location of plants coupled with the cunning planning and appropriate design of the useful features in a garden. For many gardeners this achievement alone will provide sufficient satisfaction. But for totally committed romantics, that atmosphere can serve as a background for

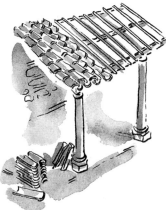

ROMAN TILES
Closely set rafters support the tiles' curved bottoms, with the narrower end of one overlapping the broader end of the tile below.
Overlapped inverted tiles are laid over the adjoining edges of the underlayer.

VASES, POTS & URNS
Since vases, pots and urns will be used as focal points in the romantic garden, they should always be attractively designed and made of high-quality materials. It is better to have one really good eyecatcher than three inferior models. Urns have particularly romantic connotations: in the ancient world they were vases, with lids, made to preserve the hearts or ashes of heroes.

their most dramatic effects, making features – which, in other circumstances, might seem merely ludicrous – highly effective and enriching. Apart from any aesthetic pleasure which their garnishing offers, features – like the obviously man-made statuary or temples, quasi-natural constructions like grottos or more natural features like rocky outcrops or caverns – serve other roles. Sited so that they are only half seen from a distance, they can stimulate curiosity and act as a lure. Nearly hidden so that they are stumbled upon by accident, they can offer a sensation of astonishment and surprise and, if the image they project is forceful enough, even induce a mild sense of shock. And either by the appearance and arrangement of the features themselves, or inscriptions which they carry, they can provoke us to think about less mundane things, or merely act as fuel for our flights of emotional fancy.

VASES, POTS & URNS

The main role of large pots, vases and urns is to command attention and draw the eye along vistas, or to provide attractive vertical features that relieve rather flat areas of a garden. They can also serve as sentinels, marking the foot or head of steps or decorating entrances and exits. If they figure classical relief work or are of a particularly elegant form, they can suggest that the garden was formerly occupied by people of noble spirit, who lived in a grander world.

In a formal garden, pots and vases are best left unplanted to allow their purity of form to be perfectly displayed. In a romantic garden they can act as a home for trailing plants, such as lobelia, ivy-leaved geraniums, or trailing convolvulus, which spill over their rim and soften the harshness of their stone. While formal gardeners strive for completeness, a slight decadence –

RIGHT This wonderfully weathered stone vase, with its slightly decrepit plinth emerging from a tumble of lady's mantle, is undeniably romantic. The wide irregular setting of the paving reinforces the effect.

indicated by a chipped base or, in the case of an urn, a broken lid – seems more acceptable in romantic situations.

Authentic eighteenth- and nineteenth-century stone or lead urns and vases are expensive. Fortunately there are plenty of affordable and attractive reproductions available in simulated stone or lead-packed fiberglass reinforced resin. Even some of the very cheap but classically shaped vases in plastic can be given a coat of primer and then a layer of ground stone in an adhesive to make them look very acceptable. Given a choice, you should choose vases and urns displaying other-worldly images, such as the busts of gods, or the heads of goats as handles, or those decorated with reliefs of the cozier themes from classical mythology.

In a hot climate, terracotta amphorae in rusting iron stands, Ali Baba jars and generous earthy pots whose forms are identical to those made by the ancient Greeks and Romans all have extremely romantic connotations. Even in cooler climates, such pots, placed on patios or terraces and in other sunny positions, will bring an evocative Mediterranean air to the garden, and endow it with the spirit of the ancient world.

STATUES

Because in a strange, petrified way statues suggest other human presences in a garden, we are always more curious about them than we are about any other dramatic artefact. For this reason you should choose them with special care other- wise, if inappropriate, they could destroy the whole romantic mood.

Modern statuary should have overall lines that are soft, but it is important to avoid works that are too winsome. When selecting among themes from mythology and literature, unless the scale of the garden is massive enough to support the notion of great heroics, it is safer to choose less overwhelming subjects. Sad lovers like Heloise and Juliet are the type of heroine whose plight we can understand and who have all been portrayed at their most beautiful. They are probably more

acceptable in a romantic garden than the equally stunning Salome, who can't be thought about without conjuring up a vision of John the Baptist's severed head. Among the gods, the friendlier ones like Bacchus, peering mis- chievously from shrubberies, will seem more at home than a blustering Mars; and, clearly, a shepherd with his crook is more likely to provoke pleasing nostalgia for an idyllic past than an early steel worker with sledge-hammer aloft about to smite iron.

If the garden is small, the work should be fairly small-scaled so as not to overwhelm its surroundings. It may also be possible to deceive an observer into believing that it is large since, if no other visual comparison is available, it is often difficult to distinguish between a small object close at hand and a large one far away.

Whatever subject is chosen it will need a mounting which is in harmony with the nature of the work and which, at the same time, marries well with the area in the garden in which it is

ABOVE Bright fronds of fern in the foreground contrast strongly with the dark water in the shadow beyond and make a perfect setting for the quizzical imp peeping out from a screen of ivy tongues. When a feature like this is finally noticed it will always provoke surprise and the slightly unsettling notion that you have been being watched without being aware of it.

located. Just as a picture must have the right frame, a sculpture needs a suitable plinth. The selection of its material and shape will be dictated both by the work itself and the nature of the materials in its surrounds. However, to impart a pleasing unity between the work and the garden, as far as possible plinths should be made from the same material as nearby masonry – brick if the walls are brick; stone if they are stone.

A statue or piece of sculpture needs thoughtful siting if its full potential impact is to be realized.

Ideal places are at the end of a pathway or long vista, or at the intersection of pathways. There the sculpture will lure attention, especially if mounted on a fairly high pedestal or plinth.

If there is a feature beyond the garden walls whose presence prevents the romantic atmosphere of the garden being enjoyed fully, you can use the sculpture to negate its worst effects. Place the work at or near the point at which the monstrosity can be seen most clearly and attention will be distracted to the work of art.

Alternatively, if the sculpture is large and impressive enough, place it so that it obscures the clearest view of the unwanted object.

Sculpture can also be displayed most satisfactorily in niches in walls that are made for that very purpose, and there are many works specially designed or particularly appropriate for displaying on walls. But there are some subjects like sprites and gorgons that are also very effective when nearly hidden among rocks or foliage. Their bizarre shapes often have more in common with those of forest plants than with human forms. Straggling Medusa hairstyles and fulsome beards mimic tangled stems, stubby horns and pointed ears could be mistaken for leaves, and the similarities will increase if they become encrusted in moss, in dark and damp places alongside, or as part of the decor of, concealed springs or rocky caverns. Sited correctly they should be overlooked by casual observers so that, when seen lurking in the shadow of ferns, their presence is all the more startling.

Particular subjects simply demand appropriate siting. Dido and Aeneas for example, should always be given a home in a cavern or a grotto, because legend has it that that is where they consummated their affair. And clearly Helios has to be given a spot in the sun. St. Dorothy, one of the Saints associated with gardening, should be given a lovely warm niche overlooking one of the most fragrant and romantic areas of the garden, where her benign presence will always be obvious.

TEMPLES

Temples large or small are among the most attractive features in romantic gardens, no matter whether their columns are made from the simplest angle iron or the most costly cut stone, if they are topped by lead-covered domes or merely a simple wood or metal open superstructure or their base plan is hexagonal, octagonal or circular. They can be bought at all prices, in all shapes and sizes, so it shouldn't be difficult to obtain one to suit any garden.

LEFT *The delicate foliage and twig tracery of a European white birch complement the precise classical lines of this little 18th-century temple. With its lovely proportions it seems dedicated to harmony and sweet reasonableness – an idea sustained by the joyful mounds of* Caltha palustris *which border the approach path.*

FAR LEFT *A perfectly sited temple seen under ideal conditions, beckoning for attention across placid reflective water through the natural archway made by a tree bough. Few of us are rich enough to contrive a similar idyll, but all of us can try to understand the vital ingredients of romance and use them on a smaller scale.*

Often a temple will be the largest structure on the land apart from the house itself, and it will contribute the right romantic atmosphere if it is as remote from the house as possible. In a small garden you can screen it from the house with a trellis or tall hedge; in a larger garden it can become the object of a walk or pilgrimage. Temples can seem equally romantic sited among trees – where their presence might be surprising – or as the centerpiece of an open glade. You can decorate the exterior with a handsome climbing plant or two – a large-leaved ivy, grape vine, wisteria or climbing hydrangea looks well, used in this way. Inside, the temple needs only to be paved a step or two higher than the surrounding land, and can include a simple seat, such as a semicircular stone bench. If you want it to appear more like a shrine, use it to house a statue.

You can even exploit the opportunities that trees offer to create natural places which have a distinctly nonsecular feeling. Evergreens, like cypresses, fastigiate junipers or yew, planted round the circumference of a circle approximately 5m/16ft in diameter will, as they grow, enclose an area which develops the characteristics of a round temple. In a larger garden you can plant deciduous trees, like feathery-leaved *Albizias* or quick-growing sycamores, at 2.5m/8ft intervals to form squares. When they reach 3.5m/12ft they can be cut and trained on wire and poles so that from then on they only grow laterally, forming a solid roof canopy. When in full summer leaf, on a bright day, the temperature in the heavy blue shade beneath the canopy will be much lower than that outside. It will be a fine place to sit and rest, having all the qualities of a sacred grove used for worship by our ancient ancestors.

FOLLIES & RUINS

Follies are, by their very nature wonderfully romantic. The aim of having them is to convey the impression that the creeper-clad relics of masonry that remain standing among piles of fallen stone were once part of some redoubtable

castle or serene monastery; that the site – instead of just being the corner of a garden – is saturated in history.

As general guidance, the ruin-maker attempts to re-erect as much or as little of the masonry as is necessary to convey the impression that there was once a large or romantic building on the site. A good way to do this is to make a ruined-looking corner from two half-built walls at right angles; something rising above the eye-line is all that is necessary. If one of the walls is developed a little at that height, the suggestion of a former window can be created by edging the wall with stone surround and even inserting a stone window arch. (You can often obtain parts of Victorian-Gothic or mock-Tudor windows, with stone surroundings and mullions, from demolition contractors.) Inadequate masons need have no fear that the corner will collapse, because

ABOVE Rather grand-looking fragments of other buildings have been reassembled to make the ruins of what might have been a palace or a monastery. The drama has been increased by allowing ivy to clamber over them. The thickly planted, unevenly sheared box is also appropriately reminiscent of mounds of collapsed masonry.

A TEMPLE PORTICO
You don't need to build a complete temple to give the impression that you have one in your garden. Simulated stone replicas of columns and other classical architectural details can be assembled against a wall to make a portico. Such features appear best as the relics of another age; stonework can be deliberately damaged, and plants grown in the cracks and up the columns.

FRAGMENTS OF THE PAST
Stones arranged to appear like old foundations, fragments of columns or scraps of mosaic paving, all half-obscured by vegetation, are simple ways of suggesting ancient grandeur in the smallest garden.

it can be supported inside, to much of its height, by cement-bound rubble, littered with a layer of loose rubble on top to disguise the reinforcement. A similar spill of loose displaced bricks or stone can be heaped round the ruin base. It will act as a marvelous home for the common English ivy, *Hedera helix,* which is the best plant to make the instant ruin seem authentic quickly.

There are firms that will supply reconstituted stone elements from which whole large-scale rectangular temples with colonnaded porticos can be built. Most gardens are too small to take the whole temple, but many could take a folly built from its components. The portico alone can be erected in front of a high wall onto which has been built an impressive false door. This piece of *trompe l'oeil* will then convince observers that the garden wall is the front wall of a chapel which continues beyond the garden margin.

The same components, when worked on with chisels and grinding wheels to crack and age them, can be used to make the portico and part of the walls of a freestanding ruined temple. Planting pockets, to take ferns and small plants such as liverworts or beauties like the Cheddar pink, *Dianthus gratianopolitanus,* or even shrubs like buddleia, can be cut high into masonry. This, in turn can be given a good coating of yogurt, manure or silage effluent to discolor and age it, and encourage the rapid development of mosses and lichens.

You can create less grand but equally effective echoes of the past by making what appear to be a couple of courses of cut stones, forming a corner, to obtrude into the edge of a pathway. This gives the impression that more of the foundations of an ancient building might be seen by digging into the undergrowth. Occasional fragments of stone mosaic or Roman brick paving set into the grit of a pathway can also suggest that the garden might have been the site of a Roman villa. This effect can be exaggerated if an odd stone classical capital or the barrel of a stone column is also allowed to emerge from a thick patch of groundcover plants nearby.

TROMPE L'OEIL

Other tricks of *trompe l'oeil* can be used successfully in romantic gardens so long as they are not too rigidly treated, and they are best if only viewed from a single place. They are usually most successful if noticed after the mind has been conditioned to accept them by the recent experience of viewing a similar but genuine structure. A good example is the placing of a trellis pergola not far from a boundary wall. From the point at which the observer emerges from the pergola, the path should be made to continue to the foot of the wall, and reduced in width by gradually inclining its sides toward its central axis. The wall will then appear to be deceptively distant. Furthermore, if a two-dimensional arched trellis structure is fixed to the wall on either side of the path, with further arches set inside it, it will seem at first glance like another pergola. Of course, to be really successful, just before visitors are tempted to walk toward it, their attention should be distracted and drawn to another object which lures them along another path at right angles to the track through the pergola from which they have just emerged.

MIRRORS, ORBS, CRYSTALS & PRISMS

You can also play *trompe l'oeil* tricks with large sheets of outdoor mirror, orbs made of mirrored glass, crystals and prisms. All of them can in some way help to extend the dimensions of the garden and widen the experience of anyone walking there. Mirrors do it by simple reflection of the area they face. This provides the optical illusion that the area is doubly large. It works best when the mirror itself is very extensive and its presence is disguised.

One way of disguising the mirror is to cover it with trellis-work supporting climbing plants. Another good trick is to make a deep false doorway in a wall and back it with outdoor-grade mirror. You can then fix an open-work iron gate in the doorway, leaving room for a few plants between it and the mirror. Visitors glancing at the doorway, seeing some of the foliage sticking through the iron gate and the reflection of the garden in the mirror, will think that they are looking into an extensive portion of garden beyond the wall.

But the value of mirrors in a romantic garden has less to do with trickery than it has with the strange, and sometimes exciting ways in which they can reflect sunlight into unexpected places. They can, for example, illuminate the underside of thick tree canopies, providing effects that are extremely theatrical. Even a small piece of mirror hidden deep inside a rocky cavern, when seen from the cavern's mouth reflecting the garden, will prompt the surprising notion that somewhere underground there is a mysterious gardened glade.

Internally mirrored glass orbs were a feature of the more bizarre sections of some eighteenth-century pleasure gardens. They can still be obtained, and if simply mounted on thin metal stalks among plants or hung from tree branches, will reflect disturbing distorted images.

Apart from the implication that glimpses of the future might be seen in their depths, the perfectly spherical optical crystal balls beloved of fortune tellers were often, in the past, used as a garden ornament in their own right – and can be so used today. They were sat in shallow depressions, made to prevent them from rolling about,

MIRRORED ORBS
Orbs of mirrored glass make fine features mounted on stalks. Resin-bonding them onto the top of metal tubes set in concrete works well. They act as eyecatchers and reflect mysterious images of the garden and a cloudy sky.

CRYSTAL BALLS
Mounted on stone columns, fortune-tellers' crystal balls make attractive features when seen from a distance. The bright transparency of the crystal seems to glow even in dull light and peering into its depth offers strange bright distortions of the garden scene.

MIRROR EFFECTS
A false gateway backed by a mirror, with plants in between them can make a garden feel more extensive. Reflected views make it appear that the garden extends well beyond the wall. The real foliage mingling with the images sustains the deception.

MOUNTED PRISMS
Prisms break light into its component colors and can change the hue of plants or masonry. As the sun moves, so the effects change.

on small stone slabs. These were mounted upon stone columns – making them look a little like sundials – at a height convenient for most adults to peer into their depths without having to lift them. The smooth surface of transparent glass contrasts wonderfully with the rougher texture of the opaque stone of the column, making an interesting feature which will often dazzle in sunlight. In different lights, surrounded by many-colored flowers and vegetation at different seasons, or under changing skies, the images in the crystal viewed from different angles are endlessly varied and fascinating. So that pausing at a crystal, which is best set on the edge of a path or given a solitary position in a clearing, can offer a refreshing and stimulating vision of the world.

In similar situations, perfect optical prisms, usually set in forged iron and mounted on a stone column, can offer equally unusual perceptual experiences by breaking light into its rainbow of components. Perhaps the nicest thing about these optical features is that they are not expensive and you can introduce them into practically any garden, and especially into small ones.

POOLS, BASINS & FOUNTAINS

No notional Eden would be complete without a spring to supply vital water, or a placid, mirror-reflective, mysterious pond with its hints of sensuous immersion and its flower-girt edge and promise of aquatic life. And in warm weather, the splash of water falling back onto a calm surface from a simple plume fountain or wall spout, with its refreshing effect upon the surrounding atmosphere, can greatly add to the appeal of a romantic garden.

But there is a deeper thrill, too, in relics of what seems once to have been a rather formal

LEFT Hostas, tree peonies and variegated ivies make a dramatic background for this charming water feature. Jets from the frog's mouth have encouraged so much moss growth that the details of the low relief sculpture on the stone slab are beginning to be hidden, which makes it seem as ancient and mysterious as the cave drawings of prehistoric man.

RIGHT A perfectly constructed romantic cascade in which the rocks are arranged to break the stream into a hundred watery tresses. It could be the setting for a thrilling Wagnerian aria or something as appealing as the resting place of an Arcadian shepherd.

pool, with cut stone margins being forced out of place by plants like saxifrages and ornamental grasses growing between them. Under these circumstances it is surprising that a simple jet should still be thrusting its plume of water toward the sky. But in this romantic atmosphere, the perceptive would be in a state of mind to understand what Siegfried Sassoon meant when – seeing such fountains in the gardens of the Villa d'Este in Florence – he compared them to the ghosts of cypresses.

All this makes water an essential element in every successful romantic garden. But the scale and way in which it is employed in any particular design will have to be dictated by the size of the plot. In a small garden, it is not necessary to have anything too elaborate in the way of a water feature. Something as simple as a hollowed bamboo spout dribbling water into a shallow, shell-shaped basin cantilevered from a wall, and which has become festooned with ferns and liverworts enjoying the damp, can have a wonderful impact.

In slightly larger gardens, you can normally find space for a small pool. It is important that the lining and edges be made to appear suitably romantic. The most satisfactory linings are those made as a single 'shell' from fiberglass reinforced plastic resin. They should be given a coat of matt-black, pond-lining paint, which is by far the best color for the base of a romantic pool because it turns the whole pool surface into a reflective mirror. You can create shallower marshy areas by piling earth behind a stone barrier inside the margin of the pool until its surface rises slightly above that of the water. Leave small gaps in the stone barrier to ensure that the earth remains constantly damp enough to support the lovely range of marsh plants, like irises, marsh marigolds, bullrushes, and plumey astilbes, which can do so much to emphasize the romantic atmosphere in a garden. You should take care to see that pools are not too heavily overshadowed otherwise they will become too infested by algae.

It is often more romantic to site pools some way into the garden, or at least to hide them slightly, where they can be encountered with surprise. Some element of trickling or running water can also increase the romantic atmosphere, and so their overflow pipes can lead directly into a deep sump hidden underground, from which water can be recirculated to the pool via an immersion pump. Instead of being returned directly to the pool, this water can be made to flow through a narrow thick-walled concrete channel set in the ground surface and disguised below pieces of rock and pebbles. In places it can be allowed to flow freely as a stream, in others it can be made gradually to bubble through a thick layer of coarse pebbles as a rill. Such a feature can greatly add to the enchantment of following a path through a thicket before arriving at a pool.

CAVES & GROTTOS

No truly ambitious romantic gardener of the eighteenth or early nineteenth centuries would have been happy without a hermit's cave or grotto – indeed some would even go so far as to employ servants of suitably shaggy appearance to act as hermits to inhabit them and impress – or frighten – their visitors.

In modern romantic gardens, simple caves can be made fairly easily by piling large, long stones against a wall in an arch shape, setting them in cement and making further, similar arches cemented to the first. These were the sort of places which hermits would have built for themselves, in which to contemplate weighty matters sheltered from hungry beasts. To make

them seem more like caves and less like constructions, they can be covered with soil and sown with ornamental grass, only leaving some of the outer rock exposed near the mouth of the cavern. By careful planting you could even make such a cave resemble Calypso's cavern where, according to Homer, 'Trailing round the very mouth of the cavern, a garden vine ran riot, with great bunches of ripe grapes, and in soft meadows on either side the iris and the parsley flourished'.

In its simplest form a decorative grotto can be made from a modified alcove, of the type shown in the illustration, which even an amateur can attempt. First, using rubble and larger stones you can make a rough rectangular shape with one curved end like a burial mound on the ground. Onto this press firmly a thick layer of moist potter's clay, which you can model with a wet trowel until it becomes a shape which fits into an alcove.

While it is still soft, you can press the hollow side of sea shells into the clay, until the surface is completely covered. Small shells can be used to fill the gaps between the larger shells and if you want to, you can arrange shells of different types

LEFT The notion of a stream slowly meandering through a meadow always has romantic connotations. Here the juxtaposition of the water and the sward has been made more obvious by having the water level only marginally lower than the edge of the mown lawn.

TOP RIGHT A man-made grotto surrounded by fern- and ivy-clad rocks, with its intriguing dark watery interior, brings an almost Gothic air of mystery to the garden.

AN ALCOVE GROTTO
*Good amateur masons can
have fun by making
themselves a pretty shell-
lined grotto as part of a wall.
First, the alcove shell is
made as detailed in the text
here and on the previous
page (top).*

*When suitably cleaned up,
the front edges of the alcove
grotto should be supported a
brick's width back from the
face of a double low wall.
The remainder of its curved
bottom should rest on a firm
concrete base of the same
height, which will stand
behind the wall. Once the
alcove is in place, the rest of
the wall can be built up
round the alcove.*

to form attractive patterns, with central designs and strongly colored smaller shells to form borders.

When they are all in place, the shells are covered with a layer of stiffish cement which has been reinforced by the inclusion of a fine aggregate. This is then covered with a sheet of fine wire mesh. And before the first layer of cement has set, a further layer is pressed onto the outside of the mesh ensuring that it coalesces round the wire with the layer below.

After leaving it for two days under damp burlap to allow the cement to cure, the alcove shell can be gently levered away from its clay

base and stood upright to allow all the residual clay clinging inside the shells to be hosed away, revealing their enticingly pearly inside faces.

You can have fun as well as romance if you attempt to create this grotto yourself. Think of the joy of collecting all those shells, the seafood suppers and clam bakes attended or given for the exotic sea snails, winkles, oysters and mussels which would have to be consumed to obtain the raw materials. And all that riotous splashing about with clay and cement, or the sheer wonderment and sense of satisfaction when the glittering interior of your alcove grotto is ultimately revealed.

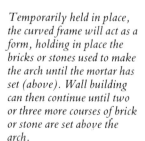

*The ends of a single layer of
bricks or stones should
project in front of the
alcove's rough concrete edges
to mask them (above). A
piece of flexible plywood can
be made into a curved frame,
with the arched front of the
alcove acting as a guide to
the shape required.*

*Temporarily held in place,
the curved frame will act as a
form, holding in place the
bricks or stones used to make
the arch until the mortar has
set (above). Wall building
can then continue until two
or three more courses of brick
or stone are set above the
arch.*

As an alternative to a shell lining, the reinforced cement can simply be cast over the mold. And when the alcove has been set in the wall, it can be drilled and plugged in many places to take galvanized screws which are left to stand proud of the surface like bristles. These act as collecting points for thin cement thrown continuously up the inside of the alcove. As the cement drips from the screw heads it gradually builds up into intriguing stalactite shapes.

When making an alcove grotto, a rather haunting effect can be obtained by leaving a small gap high in the dome through which daylight can penetrate. It will provide an illuminating shaft of light reminiscent of a theater spotlight, which will make a sculptured bust, or any other object stationed in the base of the alcove, glow eerily. This effect is most marked if the grotto is set in one of the darker and more gloomy areas of the garden.

OUTCROPS

A site with great romantic potential is a large patch of land on a hillside. Many gardeners might simply accept its shape without first trying to find out more of what lies beneath the soil, and in many cases they would be surprised at the assets they are ignoring. The most notable among them would be the occurrence of really sizeable boulders only a foot or two down. These can only be revealed profitably if they are on fairly steep slopes.

The most useful clue to their presence is if the smooth descent of the slope is abruptly broken by a distinct hummock, which brings the surface back up to – or even beyond – the horizontal before it plunges down again rather precipitously. Working back from that steeper face by digging away all the soil and loose rock it is highly likely that a sizable boulder or a whole vein of rock can be discovered. At the least it might be a buildup of fairly big rocks. In either event its exposure can make a very romantic feature. On a smaller scale, a sizable boulder can even be bought from quarries or engineering firms and imported into the garden if no suitable outcrop already exists.

To set it off well, an attractive tree like a Scots pine or a yew could be planted high just outside one of its flanks. If you were lucky you'd be creating the sort of place where no one would be surprised to see a helmeted female warrior bursting into a deep contralto aria. And pointing that out to visitors would be a good deal less boring for them than a recital of your problems with the aphids.

OUTCROPS
A rocky outcrop in a sloping garden is a wild and romantic sight. It can be created by placing a large boulder in a suitably landscaped position; however, large rocks or groups of interesting boulders are sometimes responsible for abrupt changes in the gradient of sloping sites, and they can be revealed by investigative digging.

A TREASURE GARDEN

*Few gardens could promise such secrets as this. Tree canopies forming
natural archways, climbing roses tumbling from masonry and pillars,
fleshy-leaved hostas, sword-bladed irises and snatches of sunbathed lawn are
essential elements of the best romantic planting, in which nothing is too well
ordered or well groomed. Flints built round an old stone archway (right)
create a convincing 'Gothic' ruin in the heart of the woodland garden. It
provides a characterful, partial screen preserving some of the secrets of
another alluring area of the garden beyond.*

The achievement of the owners of this garden is really quite remarkable. It is even more praiseworthy when you realize that the whole complex is the result of the labors of just two people – brothers, who have created a truly romantic garden environment on what initially seemed a rather unpromising site.

Although the soil round the old water mill and mill house was generally fertile, the land was featureless and flat. A single, mature chestnut tree and the relics of an old orchard were the only assets. Ironically, what was the remnant of an insignificant and overgrown drainage ditch was developed into one of the garden's most notable features – a branched stream which is widened in places into large pools. The introduction of this ambitious water system, accomplished by digging a 30m/100yd channel connecting the ditch to a natural stream, overcame the handicap of a basically flat site. Any residual tedium has been banished over the years by creating vertical masonry features and by wonderfully sensitive planting.

Today, the garden offers just about everything a garden-lover could enjoy: smooth lawns, wide and rich herbaceous borders, shady woodlands, water and aquatic plants, exotic marshy areas and extravagant bog plants. There is even a formal, walled kitchen garden.

A walk through the main garden begins by passing through the eastern gate on to the largest of three lawn glades. This is bounded on two sides by tall hedges of *Cedrus deodara* and *Magnolia campbellii* var. *mollicomata*. Main features here include an almost centrally placed lily pond defining a mixed border and backing onto an

RIGHT Shade and moisture lovers, such as hostas and irises, luxuriate and produce dramatic clumps of contrasting foliage in these ideal conditions. The roses, grown to look like a pink snowdrift blown against the tree trunk, are a perfect example of how to create a romantic yet natural effect. Meanwhile, the vigorous climber Vitis cognetiae *demonstrates how to mask a wall.*

LEFT A tower folly, looking as if it has stood ruined for centuries, was built only a few years ago. It illustrates what can be achieved by amateurs with no formal training but simply the courage to try and learn by their mistakes. Here, ferns, foxgloves and other shade-loving plants thrive beneath arching trees, helping to accentuate the romantic nature of this secluded corner.

LEFT *An extravagant urn and pedestal set near the entrance to the woodland garden commands attention from several areas of the site, and marks the beginning of one of the tunnellike, mown-grass paths meandering between the trees and shade-loving plants.*

area paved with flags and cobbles, which makes the ideal setting for a lion's head water spout and basin and a pedestal sundial. On the western margin of the lawn, an attractive wall and archway gives access to the woodland garden beyond.

This area still has some of the ancient apple and pear trees from the time it was an orchard, now supplemented with camellias, rhododendrons, *Ginkgo biloba* and magnolias, with white-barked *Betula jacquemontii* providing contrast. Meandering grass tracks mown through the woodland, and edged with a dense underplanting of shade-lovers, such as trilliums, cyclamen, hellebores, ferns and a host of spring-flowering bulbs, offer intriguing glimpses through the dappled light of a remarkable 'Gothic' ruin built of knapped flint around an old stone arch.

Hidden deep in a corner of the wood is an astonishing, three-celled grotto containing two large masks of river gods. Making the grotto took the brothers two winters' work and involved hauling an enormous amount of rock the entire length of the garden in a wheelbarrow.

Linking the margin of the wood with both glades to the north are bridges, one of which is a superb replica of an old, high, humped 'pack-horse' bridge made from rounded flintstones. From its summit it is possible to glimpse, beyond an arching *Picea breweriana* and a golden weeping beech, a high folly tower complete with a viewing platform on its ruined upper floor.

The 30 × 15m/100 × 50ft kitchen garden flanks the tower and provides much of the northern boundary of the garden, while behind the house is another walled garden with raised beds containing plants with a preference for drier conditions and a 'Gothic' greenhouse for tender specimens.

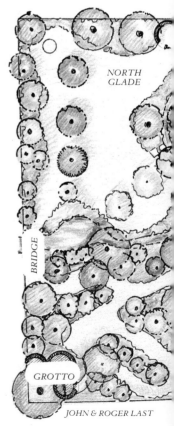

NORTH GLADE

BRIDGE

GROTTO

JOHN & ROGER LAST

Access to the margin of the mill pool on the other side of the graveled entrance to the house has been provided by a flight of steps and a poolside path. In this area you find primulas, astilbes and a profusion of other moisture-loving plants, as well as swamp cypresses and elegantly formed willows.

Taken as a whole, it would be difficult to find a better example of a medium-sized, romantic garden. Within its area of land, many of the classic romantic elements are present; archways, grottos, statues in niches, folly ruins, water, both moving and still, certainly an atmosphere of mystery in the shaded, woodland areas and, of course, a selection of plants, shrubs and trees to charm and inspire.

PLANT LIST

NORTH GLADE
Davidia involucrata
Magnolia liliflora 'Nigra'
Picea breweriana
Fagus sylvatica 'Aurea Pendula'
Catalpa bignoniodes 'Aurea'
stream-side planting of *Hosta, Primula, Astilbe, Rodgersia, Iris, Lysichiton, Caltha, Petiphyllum, Rheum,* spp.

WOODLAND
Eucryphia nymansensis
Betula jacquemontii
Juniperus recurva 'Coxii'
Metasequoia glyptostroboides
Magnolia × soulangeana
M. cordata
M. 'Leonard Messel'

M. stellata
M. sargentiana
M. campbellii var. *mollicomata*
Ginkgo biloba
Acer palmatum 'Dissectum'
Prunus serrula
Cornus kousa chinensis
C. alternifolia 'Variegata'
Cercis siliquastrum
and *Malus, Pyrus, Camellia, Rhododendron,* spp.
underplanted *Trillium, Cyclamen, Helleborus, Arisaema,* spp.

EAST GLADE & MILL HOUSE
Cedrus deodara
Prunus 'Tai-Haku'
P. × hilleri 'Spire'
Rosa banksiae 'Lutea'

Wisteria floribunda
Cedrus atlantica
Mespilus germanica
Cryptomeria japonica 'Elegans'
and *Primula, Astilbe* spp.

MILL & MILL POOL
Cupressus macrocarpa 'Lutea'
Salix alba 'Tristis'
Crataegus 'Rosea-plena Pendula'
Taxodium distichum
Morus alba 'Pendula'
Campsis 'Madame Galen'
Rosa 'Mermaid'

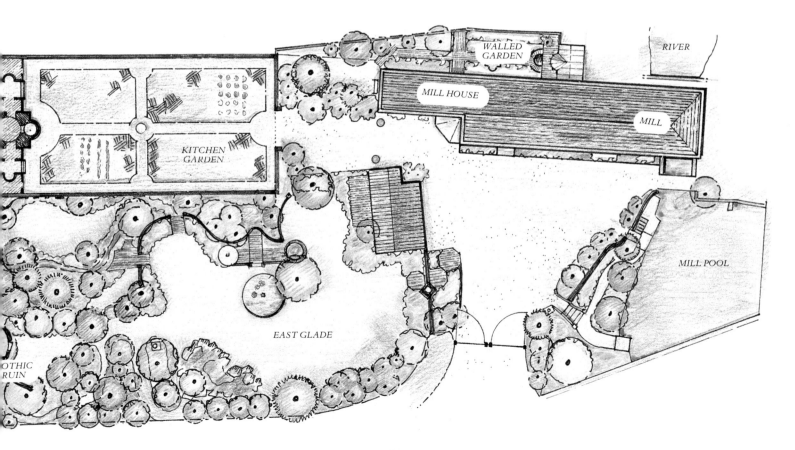

WALLED GARDEN

RIVER

MILL HOUSE

MILL

KITCHEN GARDEN

MILL POOL

EAST GLADE

GOTHIC RUIN

PLANTING THE GARDEN

Just as some garden statues, such as those of Eros or Diana, create a more romantic atmosphere than others – Caesar or Boadicea, for example – there are some plants that can imbue a garden with magical charm, and others that are overwhelmingly banal. It is a question of seeking out the real jewels, such as the small, creamy-white-flowered Scotch burnet rose, *Rosa spinosissima*, and shunning the monstrously vulgar electric-orange dahlias, with heads the size of basketballs. It is a question, too, of seeking specialist nurseries and friends, from whom one can beg seeds and cuttings of those plants which help heighten the feeling of drama or peacefulness.

Profusion and density of planting are as important as the selection and juxtaposition of particular plants, and, as a result, many areas of the garden will be partially or deeply shaded by foilage. Shade-tolerant plants will probably occupy at least half the garden, but there should be plenty of opportunity to incorporate sun-loving subjects, such as silver-leaved plants, on the edges of dense planting where there may be several hours of full sunlight on a summer's day.

In designing a garden, its hard components are assessed and used according to their architectural qualities and the emotions and associations they invoke. Plants, too, should be assessed in the same way and their structural form, the quality of their flowers, foliage and even bark considered as potential assets to the garden scene. For example, there is something enchantingly graceful about plants with slender stems which rise from a central crown and fall away, fountain-like, in arches. Some of the species roses, such as *Rosa moyesii* or the splendid, gray-purple-leaved *R. rubrifolia* provide this lyrical quality on a large scale, and complement the more brooding nature of a yew or juniper. On a smaller scale, Solomon's seal, *Polygonatum multiflorum*, or the old-fashioned, cottage-type-garden montbretia, *Crocosmia masonorum*, have this lyricism and make suitable companions for clumps of sturdy *Bergenia cordifolia*. The romantic gardener should realize, too, that plants, like people, can have characters – they can be debonair, domineering, whimsical, shy, elegant or even sinister in appearance.

Many of the plants in this chapter are species or older garden cultivars, simply because they have a modest beauty and subtle charm even though their flowering period might be briefer than the continuous blaze of color offered by many modern hybrids. The shy appeal of the English primrose, *Primula vulgaris*, and of the cowslip, *P. veris*, are prime candidates for the romantic garden. Most of the polyanthus primulas, with their frenzied riots of color and unbending stems, are best excluded.

Many of the plants included are climbers, because vertical surfaces in need of leafy concealment form the boundaries of most gardens. Then, too, climbers can be given a role similar to that of the beaded curtains hung across doorways in hot climates: creating a feeling of semiprivacy and mystery, while allowing light and flickering images to filter through.

There are climbing plants that grow both quickly and luxuriantly, and make rapid roman-

In a garden which is planted romantically, visitors should, in places, be made to feel that they are about to be engulfed by an exotic jungle. Without the experience of such intensive planting, it won't be possible for them to perceive the stimulating contrasts when moving out into an open glade. The garden shown here offers an example of such planting – it is so dense that tunnels of foliage have been created. In the darkest shade on the left, the pink blooms of Camellia 'Contessa Lavinia Maggi' glow like beacons. To its right the variegated leaves of the bamboo Sasa veitchii and the pale green of a magnolia show beautifully against the polished dark green of the leaves of the camellia. Walking a few yards along the path by the side of the pool offers an astonishing variety of plant forms, varying from the svelte blades of Iris pallida to the lacy fronds of the ferns Osmunda regalis and Onoclea sensibilis.

LEFT When herbaceous plants are used in romantic gardens they should be planted to form massive clumps and large drifts, which in summer coalesce to produce a turbulent ocean of color. As in this garden, it should never be possible to spy an unoccupied square inch of soil between them. To stand out successfully in a massed situation like this, plants either have to be large scaled, like the pale mauve campanulas (far end right-hand bed), vividly colored, like the dark blue delphiniums in front of them, have a characteristically different-shaped foliage, like the grassy crocosmia to the right of the path, or be given a very obvious location, like the silver and white anaphalis which can be seen before and beyond it.

RIGHT Here a limited spectrum of colors has been used to achieve a splendid feeling of harmony. Shades of blue predominate, with blue pansies in the foreground providing the signature which is taken up by the clear mid-blue spikes of Salvia nemorosa (top center) and the paler blue of the delphinium hybrids (top right). The sheared sphere of evergreen boxwood has been used as a foil, and the tall white flowers of Achillea decolorans and the white bells of Malva moschata 'Alba' in the foreground have been used to provide contrast and draw the eye.

tic effects a possibility. They can also present a delicate cascade of blossom, such as that provided by the old-fashioned summer-flowering jasmine, *Jasminum officinale*. On the same wall or over the same trellis or pergola, the overlapping, elephantine leaves of the ornamental grape vine, *Vitis coignetiae*, can present a sculputural curtain of green early in the season, turning to deepest red in autumn.

Although the mature garden should seem like an idyllic, thrilling spot, stumbled upon by accident, creating such a garden demands considerable forethought and planning so that all sense of contrivance is disguised. In nature, plants are never set out in rigidly geometric patterns or formal lines. All bedding plans, ribbon planting and evenly distributed plants, set out at regular intervals, are anathema to the romantic garden. So is any stretch of visible soil, particularly in the growing season.

APPEALING TO _THE SENSES_

Color and scent make perhaps the most direct and, often, poignant appeal to the senses. The novelist Mary Webb called fragrance 'the voice of inanimate things' – and some plant fragrances have haunting personal evocations, bringing to mind earlier experiences, former lovers or even certain emotional states. Sometimes one is quite suddenly confronted by the fragrance, and all that it recalls, before even seeing its source. For many of us, the heavy odor of elderberry flowers, and the pungent aroma of its crushed leaves, are redolent of childhood, when we sought its hospitable canopy as a hiding place during memorable games.

Color, too, is equally important in evoking the romantic atmosphere, but great care needs to be taken in choosing subtle tones. So many of the colors which have resulted from the miracle of modern plant-breeding techniques are brash and synthetic-looking, more reminiscent of fluorescent plastic than of nature. The presence of such colors in a garden – especially when the colors are provided by unnaturally large flowers – creates the unwelcome feeling of an airport lounge or an office cafeteria, just the kind of atmosphere from which a romantic garden is meant to offer escape.

USING COLOR

White, with its connotations of virginal purity, is always right for the romantic garden, and can be effective in adding sparks of light to dark, shady corners. Then, too, the choice of rarer, tender white-flowered forms of plants – *Wisteria sinensis* 'Alba' or the white form of annual mallow, *Lavatera trimestris* 'Mont Blanc' – adds a touch of strangeness to the feeling of romance.

Pastel pinks, blues, mauves and creamy yellows, should dominate the palette, but plants of one color are best placed together in clumps or drifts and not all intermixed. Monochromatic designs are frequent in nature and look well if copied by gardeners. Other, equally sympathetic planting plans are to select a major color theme, with one or two minor colors to add contrast, or to use several colors in drifts, which interlock where they meet.

Surprisingly, very pure, thin yellows and vivid reds can be useful, in small quantities, to add a high-key note, and prevent the romantic becoming too sweet. For example, a few small dots of intense magenta provided by the flowers of the rose campion, *Lychnis coronaria* 'Abbots-wood Rose', can hover like butterflies in front of a darker background, or add spark to a cloudy mass of white gypsophila.

Dark blues and deep purples confined to particular areas can add richness and drama, perhaps in the vicinity of a statue or other focal point. Clematis and delphiniums are good sources of blues and purples that look like velvet: *Clematis viticella; C. Jackmanii* 'Superba', *Delphinium cheilanthum* 'Lamartine', *D. elatum* 'Black Knight' and *D. elatum* 'Faust' are all good examples. Dark colors are less easily seen in a garden than pale ones, so their effect (unless grown against a white wall) is necessarily subtle, but no less romantic for it.

There is always something bizarre, but quite enchanting, about plants with green or greenish-white flowers, and it is pleasantly surprising to come across them, semicamouflaged by their surrounding background of foliage. The Corsican hellebore, *Helleborus corsicus*, and the so-called stinking hellebore, *H. foetidus*, provide pale-green, nodding, bell-shaped flowers in spring. Other green flowers include the greeny pink inflorescence of the masterwort, *Astrantia carniolica* var. *major*, the much loved and widely available *Nicotiana* 'Lime Green', and *Zinnia* 'Envy'. Technically, the strange, pale-green flowers of the spurges are not flowers at all, but bracts. In the garden, however, they do the job of flowers, lasting for weeks rather than days. Among the finest are those of the evergreen *Euphorbia robbiae*, with its leaf rosettes looking

LEFT Plants with silver foliage always have a magical tinselly quality. Even on dull days they seem to carry with them a glint of sunshine and this makes them a vital element in any romantic garden. Here an elegant white-flowered verbascum is surrounded by a group of silver-leaved anaphalis. Like many silver-leaved plants, they will have white flowers in their turn, which makes the planting of a silver and white border relatively easy.

rather like dark-green flowers themselves, and *E. wulfenii,* with its architectural, elegant, gray-green foliage.

How colors are arranged in a garden, or in a particular area of a garden, can create a *trompe l'oeil* effect. The traditional trick is to plant strong-hued flowers in the foreground, with less intense variations of those colors placed immediately behind. An exaggerated feeling of perspective is created, and so the space is made to seem much larger.

Silver plants do much to provide contrast and lightness to a darker background. They act like foil streamer theater curtains, which, at even the tiniest movement, sparkle and glitter to dazzle and enchant. The category encompasses a spectrum of textures and tones, ranging from the smooth, pale blue overlaid with a white bloom

RIGHT *White-flowered plants are always magical. Here grown to make a noble clump,* Crambe cordifolia, *with its cloud of scented white starlike flowers, is among the most romantic. Against the more solid foliage of the white rose and the sculptural leaves of the hosta below, it seems almost as evanescent as mist on a sunny morning. It is a plant to be used in an area of the garden where a lyrical mood is to be encouraged.*

of eucalyptus, to the greenish gray and woolly white of the helichrysums.

Of the 'silver' trees, the cider gum, *Eucalyptus gunnii* is fast growing, but can only be grown in the coastal north-west and the deep south. More delicate in its appearance, but also tender, is the narrow-leaved peppermint gum *E. nicholii*. The hardy white poplar, *Populus alba*, is impressively quick – perhaps too quick for the smaller garden, and certainly too greedy – but its white-felted leaves are a source of great beauty, especially when disturbed by the wind. A more suitable choice might be the whitebeam, *Sorbus aria* 'Lutescens', with its particularly silvery young leaves, or the popular and beautiful weeping pear, *Pyrus salicifolia* 'Pendula'.

Rarer, but equally beautiful and suitable for the smaller garden is the snow pear, *Pyrus nivalis*.

Its young shoots are covered with thick, white wool; both its leaves and flowers are pure white, although the leaves lose some of this whiteness as the season progresses. In Mediterranean regions, the olive tree, *Olea europea* makes whole landscapes shimmer and glisten. An alternative for colder areas is *Elaeagnus angustifolia*, sometimes called the Russian olive, though its leaves, silvery beneath, are actually willowlike.

It is, however, among the shrubs that the best silver foliage can be discovered and the most useful for small gardens. The evergreen *Artemisia arborescens* has particularly enchanting silvery leaves, like lacy filigree. The silky hairs of the bush morning glory, *Convolvulus cneorum,* seem to burnish the whole plant, and subtly complement its equally silky-looking, white-funneled flowers. There are several dwarf willows, most

107

notably *Salix lanata* and *S. repens* var. *argentea,* which have a persistent woolly coating over their foliage.

The dwarf cotton lavender, or lavender cotton, *Santolina chamaecyparissus* var. *corsica* has threadlike silvery foliage. Lavender itself, particularly the old-fashioned *Lavandula angustifolia,* sometimes sold as *L. spica* or *L. officinalis,* also has silvery needlelike leaves.

Some conifers can look very silvery in certain light, particularly hazy sunshine. *Cupressus glabra* 'Pyramidalis' is a glaucous blue, while *Juniperus squamata* 'Blue Carpet' and *Picea pungens* 'Koster' are conifers with intensely silvery blue foliage.

The choice of silver-leaved herbaceous perennials is huge, and includes many species of artemisia – wormwood, *Artemisia absinthum, A. lactiflora, A. stellerana* – as well as the ubiquitous, old-fashioned catmint, *Nepeta* × *faassenii,* often sold as *N. mussinii.*

Silver plants, on the whole, need full sun and poor, dry soil to develop their foliage color to fullest intensity. A tough silver plant is *Senecio* 'Sunshine' and it performs adequately in light shade, although its rounded foliage lacks the delicacy of some of the lacy, silver-leaved plants. The closely related cineraria, *Senecio cineraria,* is less hardy and is generally cultivated as an annual for bedding designs. Left to make its way informally through other plants, the deeply dissected silver leaves of the cineraria take on a charmingly romantic quality, and given hot, sunny conditions, the plant can grow to a substantial size.

USING FRAGRANCE

Scented plants should be evenly distributed throughout the garden, and chosen to provide their scents at different times of the year. Winter fragrance, such as that of wintersweet, *Chimonanthus praecox,* can be followed by spring scent, such as that of the double jonquil, *Narcissus jonquilla flore pleno,* and then by the penetrating scents of sweet bay, magnolia, lilacs, and roses. Autumn can provide the delicious fragrance of ripening apples and quinces, and the unmistakable aroma of chrysanthemum foliage.

The fact that some plants liberate their scents at night and others during the day should not be ignored. Evening strolls through a garden heavy with the fragrance of *Nicotiana,* night-scented stock, *Matthiola bicornis,* or any of the angel's trumpets, *Datura* species and cultivars, can be almost intoxicating experiences.

The various daphnes, such as *Daphne laureola, D. mezereum* and *D. odora,* can perfume a garden in the cool of early spring. Other plants need a

BELOW A lovely tunneled walkway has been carefully planted with a wonderful array of scented plants, so that their heady fragrance is encountered from all around. The arches overhead are clad with honeysuckle and roses, while lining the stone-paved path are sweet-smelling nicotianas, pansies and pinks, and passing feet will brush against the pretty mauve mounds of thyme.

RIGHT Sweet peas,
Lathyrus odoratus, *with their heady fragrance and almost transparent pastel-colored petals, offering us flowers for so long each season, are almost compulsory in any truly romantic garden. Although they will quickly mask any support provided for them, twiggy branches cut from hedge plants like hawthorn look more natural while they remain exposed. But in romantic situations it is much better to establish them near other shrubs, through and up which they will clamber to appear wherever they feel they can reach the light. If an early-flowering shrub is chosen to play this host role, the sweet peas appearing later will give it a second opportunity to contribute to the garden display.*

warmer atmosphere or special light conditions before their scent can be detected. The delicious spicy perfume emitted by the bark of the winter-bark, *Drimys winteri,* and the aroma of the bark of *Magnolia soulangeana,* are intensified after the wood has been subjected to several hours' direct sunlight, so the shrubs should be sited accordingly. South- or west-facing stone or brick walls act as storage heaters for the sun's warmth, and also help intensify the fragrance of nearby plants, often well into the late afternoon and evening.

Scent is always more easily appreciated in fairly still conditions, when it can linger in high concentration. This is probably why fragrance seems most intense in enclosed gardens or on calm evenings. As a general rule, there should be some scented plants near the house, and near a

heavily frequented path, or surrounding a terrace or an arbor.

Francis Bacon's dictum hints at other leafy sources of garden scent: '. . . those which perfume the air most delightfully, not passed by as the rest but being trodden on and crushed are three: that is, burnet, wild thyme and watermints. Therefore you are to set whole alleys of them, to have the pleasure when you walk or tread.' Creeping thyme, *Thymus serpyllum* and lemon-scented thyme, *T.* × *citriodorus,* pennyroyal, *Mentha pulegium,* and chamomile, *Anthemis nobilis,* can be tucked into pockets of soil between paving slabs, if the traditional herb path or alley is an impossibility.

Leaf perfumes are intensified by heat, particularly when plants are drying in the sun after heavy rain. Aromas, though, are most noticeable when the leaves are lightly handled, bruised or crushed, as Bacon noted. Just touching the foliage of lemon verbena, *Lippia citriodora*, releases waves of lemon fragrance. To Bacon's list you could add cotton lavender, *Santolina chamaecyparissus* and the looser growing *S. neapolitana*, rosemary, *Rosmarinus officinalis*, the various artemisias, bay, *Laurus nobilis*, and culinary sage, *Salvia officinalis*. Mint, in its many forms, has an intensely fresh aroma, strong enough to be sensed from some distance away; it is also one of the few herbs that will thrive in semishade. Herbs are, of course, by their very nature romantic, with their medicinal, magical and culinary ties going back thousands of years; they also tend to have pleasantly modest flowers.

The scented-leaved geraniums, although they are tender, offer a wide range of romantic scents: *Pelargonium crispum* smells of lemons; *P.* × *fragrans*, of nutmeg; *P.* 'Attar of Roses', of roses; *P.* 'Prince of Orange', of oranges; and the furry-leaved *P. tomentosum*, of peppermint. Like the herbs, their flowers are modest but enchanting.

Spicy, clovelike scents, and those reminiscent of vanilla and balsam, are almost universally appreciated. Viburnums, especially *V. carlesii* and *V.* × *burkwoodii* are excellent shrubs for spring scent. Carnations, *Dianthus caryophyllus*, and pinks, *D.* × *allwoodii*, are much loved for their clovelike fragrance in summer, which follow on after sweet William, *D. barbatus*, finishes in late spring. *Gladiolus tristis* is mildly fragrant in spring evenings, and the flowers of some of the honeysuckles, notably the winter honeysuckle, *Lonicera fragrantissima*, the common woodbine, *L. periclymenum* and the giant honeysuckle, *L. hildebrandiana*, will fill a garden with aromatic scent.

Perhaps the most evocative scent is that of roses. The basic rose fragrance often becomes overlaid with secondary scents and a collection of roses can offer a wide range of olfactory pleasures. Fragrances tend to be strongest in the older species and cultivars.

— ROMANTIC FORM —

Awareness of suitable plant shape or form plays a vital role in the creation of a romantic garden. Those that provide a sense of drama are particularly important. Some shrubs and trees – like the corkscrew hazel, *Corylus avellana* 'Contorta', or the Peking willow, *Salix matsudana* 'Tortuosa', or the contorted beech, *Fagus sylvatica* 'Tortuosa' – have a naturally dramatic form because their stems grow in a strangely contorted way, which always commands attention. Shapes like these can be useful to heighten the atmosphere of mystery or add a theatrical touch in particular areas in the garden.

RIGHT It is fascinating to speculate upon what circumstances, in the life of this Japanese maple led to its needing to adopt such a contorted form to survive. These trees always build themselves a complicated frame but this example is exceptional. It would make a wonderful feature about which to create an area of mystery in a garden; a corner that would make the experience of passing through more lyrical sections all the sweeter.

LEFT The form of flowers is also very important. Heavily romantic effects can be provided by dramatic full blooms with rich coloring, like this Iris germanica *hybrid. In general the darker the tone of the plant and the fuller its form, the greater the feeling of mystery and melancholy it will produce.*

RIGHT Hydrangeas, like this cultivar of Hydrangea serrata, *have flowers that cascade like heavy baroque necklaces. Although they are deciduous, they come into attractive foliage early in the season and their leaves persist well into the autumn. Their summer flowers blanket much of the plant until the autumn, and they do much to add interest in a garden during what is often a rather dead period. They are mound-forming shrubs which look well standing free on their own, but they also make attractive plants when grown close to a wall, where they can introduce variety to trailing or climbing evergreens set on the wall behind them.*

Nature, too, can effect her own sculpture. Often, when young, something happens to damage the leading stem of a tree and, later, several stems develop from ground level. These multistemmed trees can be beautiful and, in a landscape, a European white birch of this type can have the allure of an attractive copse. Trees can also adopt odd forms in growing. To reach light, overshadowed branches may have had to twist and turn and become much longer or more horizontal than usual. The reason for these contortions may later have disappeared – perhaps an overhanging tree has been taken down after being damaged in a storm, or has become so dominant that it needed to be removed. Left fully exposed, the strange form of the previously light-deprived tree becomes more obvious and can usually be used to supply an intriguing enrichment in a new garden design. Nearly all very old trees have some dramatic qualities and are usually worth preserving for this alone. Their heavily gnarled or corrugated bark projects characterful images that can be mistaken for the faces of gorgons or forest sprites.

RIGHT It is the diaphanous nature of the silky petals of the common poppy, Papaver rhoeas, *and the vibrance of its color which make it such a vital ingredient in a romantic garden. Although it will thrive in clumps among other herbaceous plants in a bed, it looks best scattered through a meadow lawn, where it seems to luxuriate in competition with other wild flowers and grasses sown around it. As a rule most wild flowers grow better in these crowded situations.*

RIGHT Few flowers have such full and blowsy forms as those of peonies. The sumptuous shape and intense red of Paeonia 'Robert W Austen' *will brighten even the most gloomy corner of a garden. Peonies are ideal subjects to attract attention deep into areas where a shady canopy has been deliberately encouraged to develop. Set in brighter situations the pleasing informality of their flower shape becomes more evident.*

Encountering trees with twisted forms provokes that feeling of odd surprise which makes the observer question the image. This is the type of effect that every good romantic gardener should strive to create, and, with patience, you can even make small trees with corkscrew stems yourself. The side shoots of subjects like young boxwood, *Buxus sempervirens, Viburnum tinus* or bay, *Laurus nobilis*, should be cut away rigorously as they develop, and the pliable leading stems twisted round and tied tightly to stout stakes as they grow. When they have reached the required size – usually a yard or more – you can allow their side shoots to grow and form a head. A pair of such trees stationed near the entrance to a dark shrub-lined walk will make a dramatic and slightly disturbing image, prompting visitors to wonder just what they are going to encounter next.

Fullness of form is important too, especially in flowers, where it can be soft or more flamboyant. Lovely blowsy blooms that capture affections by means of their generous scale and informality, like those of the old shrub roses, are to be preferred to the equally large – or larger – but rigid- and artificial-looking chrysanthemums or begonias. The deep crimson, cabbagey-bloomed *Paeonia officinalis* 'Rubra Plena' is suitably blowsy, as are the huge, old-fashioned Chinese peonies, *Paeonia lactiflora* and its cultivars. Similar full flamboyance is offered by the oriental poppies, like *Papaver orientale* 'Goliath' with its blood-red flowers, and the old-fashioned, slightly floppy bright orange *P. o.* 'May Queen'.

CASCADING & ARCHING SHAPES

Plants shaped like flowing waterfalls combine a feeling of movement with one of serenity, perhaps overlaid with a slight sadness, as the common epithet 'weeping' implies. Trees and large shrubs with that growth habit can also provide concealment and a venue for secret assignations, or at least the possibility of them. Children like playing inside the green nave of a weeping willow; adults can whisper endearments to each other there. Even the smallest romantic garden should have room for at least one weeping plant. The traditional weeping willow, *Salix × chrysocoma* would be too large, as would the lovely weeping linden, *Tilia petiolaris*. More suitable for a small space and equally graceful are *Salix purpurea* 'Pendula', the purple-branched, American weeping willow which eventually reaches a height of 4.5m/15ft, and the still smaller Kilmarnock willow. *S. caprea* 'Pendula', only 2m/6ft high.

The unusual weeping boxwood, *Buxus sempervirens* 'Pendula', forms a moundlike shrub, but can be trained as a small tree. Though there is no floral display, the shiny, evergreen foliage has a year-round soothing presence, and would make an ideal setting for a pale sculpture or 'antique' column at the base of its trunk.

There are several weeping forms of the spring-flowering cherry, *Prunus subhirtella*, with arching main branches and pendulous secondary branches. The single flowers of *P.s.* 'Pendula Rubra'

LEFT Few inflorescences are more romantic than the long tresses of florets offered by wisterias like those of this Wisteria floribunda *'Alba'. They emphasize the arched form which these lovely plants adopt if allowed to grow free standing or if they are merely supported to a certain height by a central frame of wood or metal.*

are small and deep rosy pink. The form *P.s.* 'Pendula Plena Rosea' has semidouble flowers of a similar color, and *P.s.* 'Pendula Rosea' forms a mushroom-shaped tree with deep-pink flowers fading to pale pink.

The butterfly-bush has cascading branches, in summer wreathed in clusters of lilac flowers. The unusual form *Buddleia alternifolia* 'Argentea' has silvery hairs coating the leaves, so that the effect, especially when seen from a distance, is that of a weeping willow dipped in silver.

RIGHT Plants with lax stems that make arching forms are essential ingredients in a romantic garden. They can be left to arch naturally as they develop, or trained and attached to the more rigid framework of another plant or support, like the rose seen here embellishing an arch formed of apple branches. Having created the archway, it is essential to have some prominent feature, such as the large clump of broad leaved rodgersias and the feathery astilbes in this garden, to lure the eye beyond the arch.

A cascading effect can also be achieved by training a climber or rambler up through a large shrub or tree, and encouraging it to hang down once the desired height is reached. Training climbers or ramblers to cascade down from the tops of wooden posts or other man-made supports is another possibility. You can even make a lovely small cascading 'tree' in this way, by pruning a wisteria or climbing hydrangea to leave just two stems, which you twine together and support as they grow (removing any sideshoots that develop), and then pruning their tops at about 2.5m/8ft, to encourage a bushy cascading 'crown'. More natural looking is a climber, such as a clematis, which makes its way to the top of a tree, such as a yew, and having reached the high branches, flows down over and beyond the dark canopy.

Wisteria, especially the Japanese wisteria, *W. floribunda* 'Macrobotrys', creates its own cascades of fragrant flowers, in racemes often 1m/3ft long. This is the wisteria traditionally trained over ornamental bridges in Japan, where racemes have occasionally reached 1.8m/6ft in length. It is perhaps more dramatic on an arch or pergola, where its flowers can hang freely in the open air, than against a trellis or wall.

Cathedrals with their soaring arches have an inspiring, uplifting effect on the spirits and in the garden, arching plants have some of that quality. Something fountaining up then returning earthward seems to follow a natural course, obeying the laws of gravity in the same way as a lobbed ball or a rocket.

The brooms, especially *Cytisus* species and cultivars, are typically arching plants. The Warminster broom, *Cytisus* × *praecox*, forms a densely branched shrub 1.8m/6ft high and as much across, covered in spring with pale-yellow blooms, white in the form 'Albus', deep-yellow in 'Allgold'. For smaller gardens, the self-descriptive 'Gold Spear' is half the size. Some people, however, find the heavy scent of Warminster broom unpleasant, and a safer choice might be the lovely, half-arching, half-prostrate

C. × *kewensis*, with cream-colored flowers in late spring. Of the *Genista* brooms, *G. lydia*, forms a low, wide-spreading mound of arching green branches, wreathed in bright-yellow flowers in late spring and early summer. It is an excellent subject for growing along the top of a wall, over which it can gracefully spill.

Fuchsias, such as the hedging species, *Fuchsia magellanica*, have pleasantly arching growth habits, left to their own devices. This is particularly pronounced in some of the large-flowered cultivars, when the branches are literally weighted down with blossom and the deep-red edible berries that follow. *Spiraea* × *arguta*, commonly known as bridal wreath, has its arching stems wreathed in blossom in late spring, like a

ABOVE Mixing vigorous and attractive climbers and wall shrubs like this is an ideal way of softening and banishing any feeling of restriction created by high boundary walls or fences. Here a vigorous climbing rose, a hybrid clematis, and the Ceanothus *'Gloire de Versailles', all vie for attention and provide a rich background for the hardy* Fuchsia magellanica *and globe-headed* Agapanthus *planted in front of them.*

RIGHT The Himalayan musk rose, Rosa brunonii has a strong fragrance and extraordinary vigor, with a capacity to put out stems which will grow to 10m/ 35ft or more. This makes these roses ideal for disguising the barriers on which they climb and enriching the whole garden in midsummer. A splendid attribute is their general hardiness and good nature. When well established, they can be cut about and generally mishandled and will recuperate quickly to make abundant stems and a sparkling froth of simple florets during the following season.

delicately hairy in *P. orientale*. Largest of all the *Gramineae* are the bamboos; the best 'all round' arching species is *Arundinaria murielae*. It is a lovely bamboo, clump-forming, noninvasive, and tolerant of dry shade. Though hardy to −15°C/5°F, its appearance is one of tropical luxuriance, and it can play a leading role in the creating of a fantasy jungle.

CLIMBERS & WALL PLANTS

For makers of romantic gardens, climbing and trailing plants are their most useful allies. They do the most to introduce a romantic atmosphere to a garden, and they are the keynote plants that tune the perceptions of visitors to a true appreciation of the spirit of the garden.

Their artistic associations are likely to invoke just the right other-worldly mood. The gentler gods or cloven-hooved fauns like Pan are nearly always figured or described with their heads crowned with wreaths of ivy. Reference to the fragrance of the woodbine – the common honeysuckle – has frequently occurred in the rural idylls of poets throughout the ages. And the grape vine, with all its Bacchanalian connotations, has served as a decorative motif and been the subject of festival since man first made the happy discovery of the intoxicating power of its fruit. They are all good climbers which can do a great deal more for the romantic gardener than simply cover ugly walls.

Apart from their masking role, their generally luxuriant and attractively shaped foliage can blur the edges of hard features, and quickly exercise the softening effect that most romantic gardeners seek. You can foster this ability because, given support – a wall, trelliswork, or even a strand of soft-surfaced wire – to which they can cling or be attached, you can lead their young and flexible stems anywhere.

The junglelike growth of climbers, even in fairly small gardens, can momentarily release us into a different, more primitive, almost tropical world; even a well-grown ivy, toughest of temperate-climate plants, has this ability. Parti-

firework explosion in white. Rarer, but worth seeking out, is *S. cantoniensis* 'Lanceata', with its long, arching sprays covered with double flowers in midspring. Its semievergreen leaves have attractive pale undersides.

Of the herbaceous perennials, there is the arching foliage of bear's breeches, particularly *Acanthus longifolius*, the relaxed, gentle overspill of clumps of catmint, *Nepeta × faassenii*, and the lofty splendor of Solomon's seal, *Polygonatum multiflorum*. Of the ornamental grasses, Bowles's golden grass, *Milium effusum* 'Aureum', provides arching, bright-yellow foliage. The aptly named fountain grasses, *Pennisetum* species and cultivars, have equally graceful arching leaves, purple in Chinese pennisetum, *P. alopecuroides*, and

LEFT *The luxuriant growth of thickly planted fast-growing ivies has completely masked the high boundary wall of this tiny romantic garden. To prevent the shady corner from seeming too somber, variegated ivies have been used, and their leaves – particularly those of the lovely* Hedera helix *'Goldheart' - seem to glow like jewels.*

cularly dramatic are the huge leaves of Canary Island ivy, *Hedera canariensis*, and Persian ivy, *H. colchica*. This in no way belittles the charm of the more modest, but hardier, *H. helix*, as attractive in the species as it is in its many cultivars. One is Italian ivy, or the so-called poet's ivy, *H.h. poetica*. Its leaves are fresh green, shallowly lobed and heart shaped, and its fruit is bright yellow. Native of the Caucasus and Asia Minor, it is naturalized in Italy, and its presence in a garden can bring echoes of the ancient world. Growing poet's ivy around the base or part-way up a classical column or statue is particularly appropriate. Ivy of any sort is excellent for providing a leafy background against which more spectacular climbers can be displayed.

Climbers that carry exotic blooms, such as the passion flower, *Passiflora* species and cultivars, or the trumpet vine, *Campsis radicans*, though very hardy, evoke visions of tropical climates. One of the most exotic looking, and suitable only for sunny subtropical areas, is the lobster claw, *Clianthus puniceus* with its ferny, foliage and racemes of brilliant-red, claw-like flowers. Like many plants often thought of as climbers, for example the winter-flowering jasmine, it is technically a scandent shrub, not a climber, but both need support and are usually trained against a wall. Other good wall plants often used like climbers are the beautiful evergreen Californian lilacs, the *Ceanothus* species.

Other unusual and highly romantic treasures for mild climates include the evergreen *Fremontodendron californicum*, with large, bright-yellow buttercups all summer long, and *Trachelospermum jasminoides*, with dark leaves that gleam like polished walnut, and fragrant, delicate white flowers. *Carpenteria californica*, with its papery white, golden-centered flowers, is a charmer when looking its best. For northern and eastern aspects, the evergreen *Azara microphylla*, with exquisitely scented, tiny yellow flowers in spring, and the deciduous *Lonicera* × *americana*, with fragrant white flowers in summer, are both splendid plants.

The ornamental grape vines are wonderfully romantic climbers. *Vitis vinifera* 'Brant', with its sweet fruit, and the crimson glory vine, *V. coignetiae*, are probably the most well known, but there are other more unusual alternatives. The parsley vine, *V.v.* 'Apiifolia', has deeply divided, handsome foliage; and the dusty miller grape, *V.v* 'Incana', has gray leaves, both surfaces of which are covered with cobweblike, white down, and against which the dark-red fruit contrasts most dramatically. The Teinturier grape, *V.v* 'Purpurea', has wine-red leaves which gradually change to deep purple as the season progresses. A statue of Bacchus in a setting of the luxuriant foliage and fruit of any of these vines would be an instantly romantic vignette.

In nature, there are no trellises, wires and eyes, and plants use each other, or themselves, to gain support. In the garden, given a bit of judicious guidance and initial tying, climbers can make their way through other shrubs or even along the ground. Honeysuckle and ivy, for example, make excellent ground cover, provided there are no delicate subjects nearby likely to be swamped by their powerful growth.

Because there are walls to be covered and most climbers lack the clinging, adventitious roots of ivies or the climbing hydrangea, *Hydrangea petiolaris*, some form of artificial support system is often necessary. Although trelliswork can be attractive, ideally, a romantic climber should camouflage its man-made support. This is even more essential for such mundane supports as wires and eyes. Many climbers, such as wisteria and ivy, in time develop thick, trunklike woody stems that are virtually self supporting, and the initial artificial support can be partially removed, if it hasn't already rotted.

In terms of year-round camouflage, evergreen climbers are obviously more effective than deciduous ones. However, the pleasure of seeing seasonal changes – new leaves emerging, growing, turning color and being shed – is lost. Also, many fast-growing deciduous climbers, such as the Russian vine or mile-a-minute, *Polygonum baldschuanicum*, and the Virginia creepers, *Parthenocissus quinquefolia* and *P. henryana*, produce such a densely tangled mass of interwining stems that they are effective camouflage even when leafless. A mixture of evergreen and deciduous climbers – indeed, evergreen and deciduous plants throughout the garden as a whole – is a sensible approach.

Some climbers need cutting back to ground level annually; they include rambler roses and the Jackmanii, Texensis and Viticella groups of large-flowered clematis hybrids. The ramblers need one-third of their oldest stems cut away immediately after flowering, to encourage the growth of new flowering wood; the clematis are usually pruned back to within 30cm/12in of the ground in late winter or early spring. Although they can be glorious in season, such plants never build up a permanent framework or presence in the garden, and perhaps should be bypassed in favor of climbing roses or species clematis, or large-flowered clematis hybrids of the Florida, Patens or Lanuginosa groups, which need less drastic pruning. Good choices would be *Clematis* 'Duchess of Edinburgh', with its rosettelike, greeny white flowers; 'W. E. Gladstone', with large, single lilac flowers and deep purple anthers; or the deep lavender-blue 'Lasurstern', with central white stamens and a second floral display in autumn.

RIGHT When fully opened the huge flat single blooms of Rosa 'Complicata' cling to its light green and abundant foliage like gigantic butterflies. In two seasons it can easily transform an attractive gateway like this into a truly memorable garden feature.

ABOVE Although bred in 1928, Rosa 'Ferdinand Pichard' has many of the characteristics of the best of the old shrub roses. It is a generous provider of its charming semidouble pink-streaked blooms over a long season. Also valuable is its vigorous growth.

RIGHT Rosa 'Le Havre' is a hybrid perpetual – hardy vigorous roses that were highly thought of in Victorian times. The beauty of its cabbagey blooms, free form and vivid color make it very appropriate for bringing brightness to a semishaded area. It would be particularly valuable set against the dark green of a wall clad in Irish ivy.

ROSES

Any romantic garden worthy of its name should contain a good selection of roses. Climbing roses, with their large scale and subtly controlled exuberance, can embellish gateways, pergolas, porches, trelliswork, arbors, walls and old fruit trees. Old-fashioned roses, both the species and their closely related cultivars, are usually more convincing in the romantic garden than modern floribundas and hybrid teas, the pruning of which leaves them looking ungainly for a long period each year.

The Noisettes – complex crosses between the perpetual-flowering China roses and the strong-growing *Rosa moschata* – are eminently suitable. They are old-fashioned, beautiful and repeat flowering. One such climber is 'Aimée Vibert', with clusters of yellow-centered, double, pure-white blooms. The dainty, scented flowers are complemented by glossy foliage. With a potential height and spread of 4.5m/15ft, though, this is a rose for a larger garden.

'Maréchal Niel' is another Noisette climber, notable for its pixielike pointed buds which open into strongly scented golden yellow blooms. It is the classic Victorian rose, with slightly nodding flowers weighing down the stems, but it needs a very sheltered position to thrive, and is some-times grown as a cool greenhouse climber for this reason. Its usual height and spread are 3m/10ft.

A third Noisette worth searching out is 'Desprez a fleur Jaune', with quartered blossom. Its scented flowers are yellow orange, overlaid with buff; it can reach a height of 6m/20ft. Equally beautiful, and much more available, is the climber 'Mme Alfred Carrière', with clusters of lovely, pinky-white double flowers. It is a good north-wall performer, notably reliable, vigorous and disease free.

Among the best species roses are *Rosa rubrifolia*, with magnificent plum-gray foliage, and small, single pink flowers followed by rich-red hips, and the vigorous *Rosa moyesii*, with long, arching stems, wreathed in single, blood-red flowers, followed by impressive, flagon-shaped hips. The latter can reach a height and spread of 3m/10ft; *Rosa moyesii* 'Geranium' is a slightly more compact cultivar with a brighter, scarlet color, retaining the charm of the species.

Rosa × *pteragonis* f. *cantabrigiensis* has beautiful ferny foliage and enormous, pale-yellow flowers produced in late spring, and is among the first of roses to bloom. It is an exuberant shrub, about 3m/10ft high and as much across, and can also be trained as a climber. Its slightly scented, cup-shaped flowers are nonrepeating, but are freely produced over a period of about three weeks. Earliest of all is the incense rose, *Rosa primula*, with small, primrose-yellow flowers and fernlike foliage smelling heavily of incense. With a height and spread of 1.8m/6ft, and a gracefully arching growth habit, it is suitable for even fairly modest-sized gardens.

Wolley Dodd's rose, *Rosa villosa* 'Duplex', the semidouble form of the old-fashioned apple rose, is a lovely candidate for the romantic garden, with blue-green fragrant foliage and pink flowers. The hips are apple shaped.

The Rugosa roses, species and cultivars, are both charming and useful. They can make a splendid floral hedge, either as a boundary marker or for internally subdividing a larger garden and single specimens can fill a corner or part of a mixed border. The Rugosas are tough, prickly and virtually impenetrable, and will grow in relatively poor conditions. They are highly disease resistant, long flowering and have very attractive, deeply veined foliage.

As well as the species, *Rosa rugosa*, with its large deep pink flowers and large orange-red late summer hips, there are three lovely cultivars. 'Blanc Double de Coubert', with a height and spread of 1.8m/6ft has open, pure-white papery flowers which begin to appear early in summer and continue until the first autumn frosts. 'Pink Grootendorst' has clusters of small, coral-salmon flowers, fringed rather like a carnation. It makes a compact shrub, 1.2m/4ft high and as much across. Lastly, the ever-popular 'Roseraie de

l'Hay', with flat, richly perfumed, crimson-purple blooms, which smell of sugared almonds, and bright, apple-green foliage which takes on lovely autumn tints before falling, is worthy of a place in any garden.

Even the names of the old-fashioned shrub roses, mostly bred in nineteenth-century France, can add romance to a garden. Though some have rather ungainly, erect growth, it can be concealed in dense surrounding planting, and their lovely flowers make them worth the camouflage. The Bourbon rose 'Reine des Violettes' has fragrant, velvety, Parmaviolet colored blooms of tightly packed petals, set off by glossy foliage. The Damask rose 'Madame Hardy' has an elegant growth habit and strongly quartered blooms with a lemony fragrance and an unusual green button 'eye'. The flowers are sometimes palest pink to start with, becoming pure white as they open, the outer petals recurving and the inner petals remaining incurved. 'Camaieux' is one of the most beautiful striped Gallica roses, with semidouble, fragrant, pale-pink flowers striped in purple-crimson. As the flowers age, the stripes gradually fade to magenta and then

ABOVE Rosa *'Albertine' is a beautiful old-fashioned-looking rambler, whose buds are salmon-colored before they open to a unique coppery pink. These strongly fragrant blooms and the rose's great vigor make it an excellent choice for a romantic covering on walls or other surfaces.*

LEFT Named 'Adelaide d'Orleans' by its breeder – who was the gardener to the Duc d'Orleans – to commemorate the Duc's daughter, this is among the best and most romantic of the classic old roses. A very strong grower, it will put out stems up to 5m/16 ½ft long with clusters of beautiful, creamy and fragrant blooms.

pale lilac. With gracefully arching stems and relatively compact growth, 1.2m/4ft high and across, it is a good choice where space is limited.

Some modern shrub roses combine the glorious characteristics of the old-fashioned shrub roses with a longer flowering period. Among the most attractive is 'Mary Rose', with rich pink flowers and a strong Damask fragrance. It is robust but compact, with a height and spread of 1.2m/4ft. It begins flowering early in the season and is among the last roses to finish.

The modern shrub rose 'Graham Thomas' is a similar size, and carries yellow flowers on slender, gracefully arching stems. The flowers are cup-shaped, densely packed with petals, and have an old-fashioned appearance and a rich, tea-rose scent. Although both 'Graham Thomas' and 'Mary Rose' can be hard pruned, in the manner of hybrid tea roses, for fewer but larger flowers on a smaller bush, the plants look more informal (and romantic) if allowed to assume their natural size and form.

USING FOLIAGE

Variety is one of the key factors in creating interest and mood in any garden. Plants with dramatic foliage should be included, but always partnered and balanced by those with a more delicate or modest appearance, to allow the sheer luxuriance of the former to be fully appreciated.

In terms of luxuriance, trees with large, palmate leaves, such as the horse chestnut, *Aesculus* species and cultivars, always catch the eye. Most horse chestnuts, though, are too big for ordinary gardens, although the shrubby *A. parviflora*, with a height and spread of 3.5m/12ft and typically lush horse-chestnut leaves, would make a dramatic focal point without overshading vast areas of ground.

The Indian bean tree, *Catalpa bignonioides*, and the princess tree, *Paulownia tomentosa*, have huge, oval or roughly heart-shaped leaves. Both form large trees, but may if necessary be cut back annually to ground level. Though neither will flower under this regime, they will produce a vigorous coppice of stems. The castor oil plant, *Ricinus communis,* has highly polished exotic-looking palmate leaves, combined with a tough constitution. This Victorian favorite grows fast and is trouble free. It can fit equally well in an ultra-modern garden or an old-fashioned, romantic one – as can the common fig, *Ficus carica*, which provides sculptural, pale stems, unusual, lobed leaves, and ripe fruit, given hot summers and a sunny, sheltered spot.

Used sparingly, spiky shrubs are valuable for contrasting with softer forms, or drawing your eye to a feature or focal point. In milder areas, the New Zealand flaxes, *Phormium tenax* and its many-colored cultivars, offer decorative spiky foliage on a grand scale, up to 3m/10ft high in the form 'Goliath'. For tiny gardens, the cultivar 'Thumbelina' produces bronzy-purple foliage only 30cm/12in high; most, though, have foliage about 1m/3ft high.

For gardens in colder areas, the various species of *Yucca* have the same tropical overtones, though they are very hardy, given full sun and free-draining soil. Among the best are the variegated *Y. filamentosa* 'Variegata', with creamy white stripes, and spikes of large, white, bell-shaped flowers in early summer.

There are many plants with the romantic air of old lace, with delicate, airy foliage for intermingling with more dramatic subjects. The cut-leaved silver maple, *Acer saccharinum* 'Laciniatum', combines a lovely pendulous habit with deeply incised leaves, silver on the undersides and bright yellow in autumn. The rowan, or mountain ash, has a cut-leaved form, *Sorbus aucuparia* 'Aspleniifolia', with fernlike leaves. The thornless honeylocust, *Gleditsia triacanthos* var. *inermis* can provide feathery light shade, which allows a rich variety of understory plantings to flourish beneath. Gardens in very mild areas can grow the

BELOW Plants with bold lush foliage can be massed together to give a tropical air to the smallest garden, and if the climate is harsh many can be grown in pots and kept inside in winter. Here, the effect of the elephantine leaves of Gunnera manicata, *and the grassy foliage of the underplanted* Phalaris arundinacea *'Pieta' is made even more exotic with pots of* Agave americana *'Marginata' and the decorative banana,* Musa coccinea *'Marginata'.*

florist's mimosa, *Acacia dealbata*, with its very beautiful scented yellow flowers which appear in very early spring. Its downy, pinnate foliage is as delicate looking as its fluffy flowers.

Herbaceous perennials offer an equally wide range of foliage, on a smaller scale. Those with dramatic foliage include members of the *Acanthus* genus, the deeply ribbed *Hosta sieboldiana*, and the umbrella plant, *Peltiphyllum peltatum*, which produces large lobed leaves, like parasols on 1m/3ft high stalks. The Iris family and red-hot pokers, the genus *Kniphofia*, provide spiky foliage as valuable as their various flowers. For small-scale lacy foliage, ferns provide a wealth of choice. Particularly dainty are the lady ferns, *Asplenium felix-femina*; there are named forms with crested, subdivided and feathery fronds. And there is a hardy maidenhair fern, *Adiantum venustiem*, which will form a lacy evergreen carpet in cool shade.

LEFT *A small grove of the* stags horn sumach, Rhus typhina, *makes an enchanting feature which can be established very quickly. In full leaf its canopy is sparse enough to allow sunlight to penetrate, making an intriguing shadow-play on the ground. In autumn the foliage flares to a flaming orangey red. Even when the leaves have fallen, the knoblike seed heads, which remain on twigs branching like stags' horns, give the tree a strange and altogether different allure. Many of these characteristics are 'lost' when it is used in a mixed planting.*

WATER & WATERSIDE PLANTING

Water plants derive their romantic appeal partly from their form and partly because of their proximity to water, which always has the potential to evoke a calm, peaceful state of mind. No Arcady would be complete without the life-sustaining, cleansing presence of water, and its promise of soothing refreshment.

Water plants are often reflected in the water surface, which doubles their visual presence in a garden and adds a touch of slight unreality, especially when the sky as well as the plants is reflected. Together with this teasing, 'double-take' quality, water plants also benefit from the particular light associated with a reflective water surface. Waterside plants sometimes take on a dramatically silhouetted appearance, seen against a bright foreground or background of water. At other times, mist rising from the water gives a ghostlike quality to the surrounding plants, softening their colors and forms.

Of the deep-water aquatics, the hardy water lilies are the most obviously romantic, although some do border on the unnaturally perfect and waxlike. Their habit of opening at midday, in response to the sun, and closing at sunset is a charming one. Among those with white blooms, *Nymphaea alba* although exquisite, is too vigorous in all but the largest pools. A good alternative for medium-sized pools is *N. candida* var. *wenzelii*, which produces small, star-shaped white flowers with bright-yellow centers. For water less than 30cm/12in deep, in tubs and sink gardens, or the shallow shelves bordering deep pools, *N. odorata* var. *minor*, with diminutive, heavily scented white blooms, is ideal. Tiniest of all, with flowers 2.5cm/1in across, is *N. pygmaea* var. *alba*.

The full color range of hardy water lilies is very wide, with only blue missing from the palette, although there are tender tropical species and hybrids with blue flowers. The colors can add to a feeling of idealized wilderness in the garden, or create a gaudy confusion, depending on the restraint with which they are chosen and

RIGHT Zantedeschia aethiopica *'Crowborough' will luxuriate in boggy areas at the edge of a stream or pond and in shallow water making great clumps of luscious dark green foliage topped by pristine white trumpets. The form of the classic arum lily is so outstanding that for centuries it has appealed to painters and tapestry designers who have used it to reinforce romantic themes.*

BELOW Growing with their roots in the habitually damp soil of the waterside, the reddish pink Astilbe *'Etna' and the clear pink* A. *'Rheinhard' develop into vast thickets. Here they make a spectacular jostling background for the calm dark green of the water lilies.*

juxtaposed. Unless the water surface is a large one, it is probably better to stick to a single color, or variations on a theme, such as light and dark pinks. Among the most seductive are the deep-pink, orange-centered, fragrant flowers of N. 'Firecrest'.

The purple young foliage and peonylike crimson flowers of N. 'James Brydon' make it a superb choice for medium-sized ponds, while the wine-red N. 'Laydekeri Purpurata' is ideal for tub culture or tiny pools. This hybrid begins flowering in midspring and continues, non-stop, until cut by frost. The orange-red stamens that fill the center of each bloom and the maroon-flecked leaves create an intense color combination, one which benefits from expanses of visually cooling greenery nearby.

The yellow hues of water lilies range from the soft, glistening yellow of N. 'Marliacea Chromatella', backed by attractively mottled foliage, to the canary yellow of the miniature N. pygmaea 'Helvola'. Again, the bright-orange stamens and brown and purple-mottled foliage of the latter

BELOW Waterlily pads – which in early season look like isolated landing platforms for dragonflies – are encouraging harbingers of the glory to come, when their rafts will thicken and they will put out their glorious glistening cuplike flowers, like this Nymphaea 'Rose Arey'. *They can add a pre-raphaelite charm to even the smallest pond or an otherwise ordinary garden. Plants of placid waters, no attempt should be made to locate them in anything but the calmest streams.*

create a dramatic contrast, demanding neutral surroundings if the overall effect is not to become frenzied.

The effect of the elegant flowers and heart-shaped foliage of the arum lily, *Zantedeschia aethiopica* is overwhelmingly romantic. Although it can be grown on land, it makes more robust clumps of its shiny, dark-green leaves and pure-white spathes in water. In cold areas, arum lilies are best grown in pots on the shallow ledge of a pool. They can be removed from the pool before the first frost and overwintered in a cool but frost-free and well-lit spot. Alternatively, they can be overwintered in fairly deep water, below the likely frost level. The cultivar 'Crowborough' is hardier than the species.

Water hawthorn, *Aponogeton distachyus*, has semievergreen, straplike leaves which float like small boats on the water's surface. Its spikes of exotic-looking, waxy white flowers with black stamens produce a haunting vanilla fragrance. Water hawthorn flowers profusely, with up to two dozen flower spikes per plant, from mid-spring to late autumn. The plant is attractive but not fiercely eye catching, so it makes a suitable companion for the showier water lilies.

Of the floating plants, the tiny little floating fern, *Azolla caroliniana*, is as delicate as its name. The individual plants form lacy mats on the water's surface, and turn brilliant deep red before dying back in autumn.

There is a wide choice of water-edge plants for shallow water or very wet soil. Large clumps of fewer types look more natural, and hence romantic, than one or two specimens of many different types. In time, large groups of plants will interweave with their neighbors and boundary edges will soften, so any initial formality will disappear. Base the selection as much on contrasting foliage shapes – spiky, round, or lacy, for example – as on flowers.

The variegated sweet flag, *Acorus calumnus* 'Variegatus', has irislike foliage. The green, creamy white and pink-striped leaves smell of citrus fruit when bruised or crushed. Its tiny

RIGHT *In mild climates, the tight little valleys that surround small streams can provide really protected environments for romantic fern plantings. Here, set in the bottom of the valley, the variegated* Pteris cretica *'Albolineata' stands out wonderfully in the gloom against the dark water. Maidenhair ferns, (*Adiantum *species) clamber on the rocks above, overhung by the elegant fronds of a tree fern.*

cousin, *A. gramineus* 'Variegatus', creates tufts of grassy foliage, boldly striped sulfur yellow. The Japanese sweet flag, as it is called, will grow in shallow water as well as moist ground, providing an attractive, evergreen lawnlike edge, and is particularly useful for hiding the rim of an artificial pool.

Winter mint, *Mentha aquatica*, does an equally good camouflage job, growing as it does in shallow water or moist ground, though it does die down in winter. Its leaves have a minty aroma and it has lovely mintlike mauve flower heads. Water mint is invasive, needing to be kept firmly under control if it is not to take over completely.

The elegant Japanese water iris, *Iris laevigata*, definitely prefers its roots in shallow water. As well as the grassy leaved, clear blue-flowered species, the white-flowered *I. l.* 'Snowdrift' and the silver-variegated *I. l.* 'Elegantissima', with pale-blue flowers, are worth growing. Yellow water iris, *I. pseudacorus*, native to Europe and naturalized in the US, is rather too grand and vigorous for most gardens, and in small pools might be better represented by the form 'Variegata', with golden-striped young leaves.

Pickerel weed, *Pontederia cordata*, is far more aristocratic looking than its common name suggests. Its glossy, lance-shaped leaves are held erect, like shields, to protect its large, delicate blue flower spikes, which can be 1m/3ft or more high, and are borne in late summer.

In large, mild-climate gardens, a sense of waterside drama can be created by including the enormous *Gunnera manicata*. Its huge rounded and bristly leaves could seem primitive enough to provide shelter for a clutch of young dragons. In smaller gardens, where space is at a premium, the ornamental rhubarbs, *Rheum* species and cultivars, could be substituted. Lastly, whatever the size of garden, moisture-loving ferns, such as the ostrich fern, *Matteuccia struthiopteris*, and the sensitive fern, *Onoclea sensibilis*, are worthy of space for their delicacy and intimations of untamed nature.

A WOODLAND GARDEN

In this beautifully planted garden a stone-paved path invites inspection of areas of the garden away from the house, while the white blossom draws the eye down the vista. Large stones (right), like those in the foreground, make wonderful, natural-looking features to contrast with the abundance of flowers and foliage in a woodland setting.

130

Untouched woodland can take on a romantic, almost magical quality of its own. Anybody lucky enough to discover a sloping acre packed with lovely dogwood trees, like the owners of this garden, can by sensitive manipulation and planting transform it into an even more enchanting place.

The major difficulty to be confronted was the need to preserve the atmosphere of forest mystery while, at the same time, giving the site some sort of coherent structure and overall form, as well as providing routes and paths so that its charms could be properly appreciated.

Here, this was achieved by a thoughtful removal of only those trees and shrubs – and undergrowth – necessary to provide paths and open vistas and enable sufficient light to penetrate the leafy canopy to allow a wider range of planting beneath.

Planting and remodeling the garden went on in step with thinning and dragging out the tangle of roots. Excavation required for the clearings

Azaleas, magnolias and a cluster of annuals and perennials, including forget-me-nots and the elfin bells of lily of the valley, enrich the floral tapestry of this leafy cavern. But note how what might have become an almost-too-rich profusion of color and vegetation has been saved by the simple inclusion of the flower-shaped birdbath on its stone column.

inevitably yielded copious amounts of rock, which was used on site to create walls, raised beds and terraces to retain and stabilize the thin, forest soil.

The most intensely cultivated central area of the plot is, in reality, a series of irregularly shaped glades connected by meandering paths of mown turf. Much narrower, rough-cut, grass tracks weave through the thicker woodland margins of the garden, where much of the original planting remains, enhanced by further additions of ornamental shrubs and trees.

In another part of the garden, two boulders provide attractive flanking features for a deeply excavated lily pond with a fountain. Elsewhere, an almost-life-sized, couchant, bronze foal among the day lilies and bleeding hearts, an attractive, Victorian, cast-iron seat snugly tucked into a surrounding of evergreens, a bronze figure of a child sitting on the pond edge, a stone hare surveying the scene from a jumble of craggy boulders and a flower-formed, stone birdbath are the only hard artefacts that have been used to add interest to the garden: otherwise, it is the plants that hold center stage.

In any area like this with hot, dry summers and often harsh winters, if you wish to supplement the color of your trees and shrubs with herbaceous plants, you must be prepared to preserve bulbs and protect any perennials whose hardiness is at all suspect. But the rewards are more than evident.

In early spring, crocuses and aconites begin their display. A Persian carpet of daffodils, tulips and chionodoxa, interspersed with *Phlox divaricata* and Jacob's ladder, is overhung with forsythia, pieris, magnolias and dogwoods, all blooming in April and May.

Later in the year attention is focused more centrally in the garden, where lilies and day lilies, hostas and echinops flower against a backdrop of snowball bushes and rose-of-Sharon. Annuals that appreciate shade, such as impatiens and nicotiana, surround the pool with brilliant color.

PLANT LIST

TREES & SHRUBS
Salix spp.
Rhododendron spp., cvs.
including *R. mucronulatum,*
R. schlippenbachii, Mollis and
Exbury hybrid azaleas
Magnolia stellata
M. × soulangeana
Pieris spp.
Forsythia
Syringa
Malus
Cornus spp. including *C. kousa*
Prunus laurocerus
Hypericum calycinum
Viburnum opulus 'Sterile'
Hydrangea spp.
Euonymus alatus
Ilex spp.

BULBS
Eranthis hyemalis
Galanthus nivalis
Chionodoxa
Puschkinia scilloides
Narcissus spp., cvs.
Tulipa spp., cvs.
Hyacinthus spp., cvs.
Lilium spp.

*PERENNIALS
& ANNUALS*
Hepatica nobilis
Anemone spp.
Primula spp.
Houstonia caerulea
Dicentra spp.
Tiarella cordifolia
Polemonium caeruleum
Trillium grandiflorum
Alyssum
Viola spp.
Phlox divaricata
Myosotis
Papaver orientale
Aquilegia spp., cvs.
Iris spp.
Delphinium consolida
Achillea millefolium
Campanula
Baptisia australis
Coreopsis
Hemerocallis spp.
Hosta spp.
Astilbe
Platycodon grandiflorum
Helianthus
Celosia argentea
Salvia
Chrysanthemum spp.
Sedum spectabile

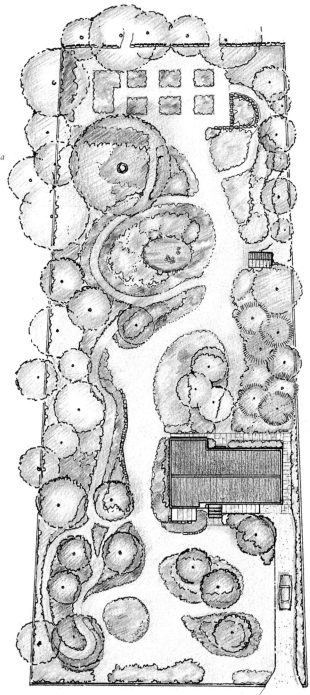

MR & MRS LEVITAN

—ROMANTIC PLANT CHARTS—

As well as the plants described in the previous pages, there are of course many more that are suitable for the romantic garden.

The plants named in the charts that follow, whether they are natural species or man-made hybrids, are the result of a careful search through the whole panoply of the plant kingdom for those with the most blatantly romantic qualities. When you are selecting plants for inclusion in a garden, every effort should be made to seek species or hybrids with this characteristic. The temptation to plant something merely because it is given by kind friends or easily available should be resisted unless you feel it can genuinely contribute toward the romantic mood that you are trying to create. Nowadays, even the great nurseries are striving to reduce their inventories by limiting the number of plant types that they offer and the discriminating gardener may have to look long and hard before finding a particular plant. However it must not be forgotten that many beautiful plants can be propagated relatively easily from soft or hardwood cuttings, or often root cuttings, begged from friends. Many shrubs and trees and a wide range of perennial, biennial or annual herbaceous plants can also be grown from seed; this is probably the most satisfactory way of obtaining the more attractive of the modern hybrids. But this technique can only be used satisfactorily if the gardeners are prepared to provide themselves with the right equipment and facilities and do the job properly.

In these charts, approximate sizes have been given for trees, shrubs, climbers and wallplants. In all cases the heights indicated are based on what you could expect your climbers and wall-plants to attain in ideal growing conditions after about 20 years. Your own conditions may of course vary. The sizes covered for each group are:

Trees: Small: up to 6m/20ft. Medium: from 6m/20ft to 15m/50ft. Large: from 15m/50ft upward.

Shrubs: Small: up to 1.2m/4ft. Medium: 1.2m/4ft to 2.5m/8ft. Large: from 2.5m/8ft upward.

Climbers and wall shrubs: Small: up to 3m/10ft. Medium: 3m/10ft to 6m/20ft. Large: from 6m/20ft upward.

Also indicated in these charts are the United States Department of Agriculture hardiness zone ratings. These give an approximate minimum temperature a plant will tolerate in winter. However, a plant's hardiness may also vary according to its original geographic source and to your local climatic conditions. Bulb hardiness zone ratings are more complex than other plant ratings, because exact information on the limits of cold tolerance of hardy bulbs is sketchy. In these charts, therefore, most relatively hardy bulbs have not been given a zone rating. In extremely cold regions, visit your local botanic garden or contact your local Extension Service for advice on which cultivars perform best.

Approximate range of average annual minimum temperatures zone
1   below −45°C/−50°F
2   −45°C/−50°F to −40°C/−40°F
3   −40°C/−40°F to −34°C/−30°F
4   −34°C/−30°F to −29°C/−20°F
5   −29°C/−20°F to −23°C/−10°F
6   −23°C/−10°F to −18°C/0°F
7   −18°C/0°F to −12°C/10°F
8   −12°C/10°F to −7°C/20°F
9   −7°C/20°F to −1°C/30°F
10 −1°C/30°F to 4°C/40°F

The symbols ★ indicating evergreen and ‡ indicating semievergreen have been used.

— TREES —

NAME	SIZE & SHAPE	SITUATION & CULTIVATION	FLOWERS/FOLIAGE	FURTHER DESCRIPTION & USES
Acer griseum Z 5	medium; rounded	plant in well-drained acidic soil in sun or half-shade	insignificant flowers. Three-lobed green leaves turning scarlet-red in autumn	showy peeling bark is a cinnamon color
A. pensylvanicum Z 3	small; open and irregular	plant in moist but well-drained acidic soil in half-shade	yellow flowers in late spring. Wide three-lobed green leaves turning bright yellow in autumn	distinguished for its erect young green stems becoming striped white and jade green
A. saccharinum 'Laciniatum' Z 3	small to medium; pendulous	plant in soil in any situation	deeply cut green leaves, with silver-white undersides, turning gold-red in autumn	quick growing
Aesculus hippocastanum Z 5	large; rounded	plant in well-drained acidic soil in sun or half-shade	erect candles of white flowers with large yellow then red eyes in spring. Leaf has five to seven palmate stalkless green leaflets, turning yellow in autumn	produces shiny horse-chestnuts in autumn
Albizia julibrissin Z 6	medium; rounded	plant in well-drained soil in sun	pink flowers in summer. Small pinnate green leaves on leaf stems	quick growing
★*Arbutus unedo* Z 8	small to medium; wide topped	plant in well-drained soil in sun or half-shade	pendant bell-shaped ivory-cream flowers in autumn. Large narrow oval dark green leaves	slow growing; strawberrylike orange-red fruit appears at same time as following season's flowers
Betula nigra 'Heritage' Z 4	medium; broadly conical	plant in sun or half-shade; tolerant of wet soils	catkins in spring. Small ovoid green leaves turning golden in autumn	dazzlingly cream stems under peeling bark
B. papyrifera Z 2	large; rounded dome, drooping branches	plant in moist well-drained soil in sun or half-shade	catkins in spring. Diamond-shaped green leaves turning yellow in autumn	peeling smooth white bark when mature
★*Buxus sempervirens* 'Pendula' Z 6	small; pendulous	plant in well-drained soil in any situation	small dark green leaves	
Castenea mollissima Z 5	large; broad domed	plant in well-drained soil in sun or half-shade	catkins in midsummer. Oblong toothed glossy green leaves turning yellow in autumn	quick growing; rich brown edible nuts; blight resistant
Catalpa bignonioides Z 5	medium; wide domed	plant in moist well-drained soil in sun	candles of white florets flecked with yellow and purple in summer. Very large heart-shaped fresh green leaves	quick growing; long green seed pods in autumn
★*Cedrus atlantica* f. *glauca* Z 6	large; conical	plant in well-drained soil in sun or half-shade	small resinous-scented blue-gray needles arranged spirally as tufts along the shoots	quick growing. *C.a.g.* 'Pendula' has weeping branches and attractive cones. Size: small

NAME	SIZE & SHAPE	SITUATION & CULTIVATION	FLOWERS/FOLIAGE	FURTHER DESCRIPTION & USES
★*Cedrus deodara* 'Shalimar' Z 6	large; conical, drooping branches	plant in well-drained soil in sun or half-shade	short resinous-scented dark green needles in tufts along stems	quick growing
Cercidiphyllum japonica Z 5	large; bushy	plant in well-drained acidic soil in sun or half-shade	small heart-shaped bright pink to sea-green leaves turning yellow with tinges of pink in autumn	sometimes multi-stemmed; fallen leaves have sweet scent
Cercis canadensis Z 5	small; upswept, rounded dome	plant in well-drained soil in sun	clusters of pea-shaped rose-lilac flowers in midspring. Distinctive heart-shaped light green leaves	quick growing; purple tinted seed pods
★*Chamaecyparis nootkatensis* 'Pendula' Z 5	medium; conical, drooping branches	plant in well-drained soil in sun or half-shade	coarse resinous-scented fleshy close-set dark green leaflets, typical of false cypress	slow growing
Cornus florida Z 5	small; horizontal branching	plant in well-drained acidic soil in half-shade	flower heads, each surrounded by four white bracts, in midspring. Oval green leaves turning bright red in autumn	
C. nuttallii Z 7	medium; rounded	as above	large white bracts, flushed with pink, in late spring. Oval green leaves turning red or yellow in autumn	best where summers are cool
Corylus avellana Z 5	small; bushy	plant in well-drained soil in sun or half-shade	catkins in late winter. Oval green leaves turning yellow in autumn	usually grown as multistemmed shrub; edible nuts. *C.a.* 'Contorta' has curious twisted branches
Crataegus viridis 'Winter King' Z 4	medium; rounded	plant in well-drained soil in sun	small white flowers from late spring to early summer. Small dark green leaves	attractive red berries persist well in autumn
★*Cryptomeria japonica* 'Elegans' Z 6	small; conical	plant in well-drained soil in sun or half-shade	finely divided furry resinous-scented brown-green foliage turning copper-bronze in autumn	slow growing
★*Cupressus glabra* 'Conica' (*C.g.* 'Pyramidalis') Z 7	medium; conical	plant in well-drained soil in sun	typical resinous-scented blue-gray cypress foliage	quick growing
Davidia involucrata Z 6	medium; conical to tall domed	plant in well-drained soil in sun or half-shade	large white bracts, protecting flower heads, in late spring once tree is at least ten years old. Broadly ovate shiny bright green leaves with paler undersides	
Elaeagnus angustifolia Z 3	medium; bushy	plant in well-drained soil in sun or half-shade	small fragrant flowers, silvery outside, yellow inside, in early summer. Lanceolate silver-gray foliage	oval silver-amber fruits in autumn
★*Eucalyptus gunnii* Z 9	large; open, lozenge-shaped	plant in well-drained soil in sun	fragrant glaucous leaves when young; adult leaves sickle-shaped gray-green	quick growing
Fagus sylvatica Z 5	large; broadly domed	plant in well-drained soil in sun or half-shade	oval strongly veined clear green leaves	silver-gray bark in winter. *F.s.* 'Pendula' has weeping branches

NAME	SIZE & SHAPE	SITUATION & CULTIVATION	FLOWERS/FOLIAGE	FURTHER DESCRIPTION & USES
Ficus carica Z 7	medium; bushy, spreading	plant in well-drained soil in sun in protected location	large flat five-lobed green leaves	edible fruits which turn purple when mature
Ginkgo biloba Z 5	large; upswept	plant in well-drained soil in sun or half-shade	fan-shaped very pale green leaves, with prominent veins, turning buttercup-yellow in autumn	quick growing; a hauntingly different and very primitive tree which has changed little in 150 million years; tolerant of urban conditions
Gleditsia triacanthos var *inermis* Z 4	medium; broadly domed	plant in well-drained soil in sun	insignificant flowers in spring. Small pinnate bright green leaves turning yellow in autumn	long twisted seed pods on female plants; male clones recommended
★*Ilex cornuta* Z 7	small; dense bushy	plant in well-drained soil in sun or half-shade	rectangular five-spined glossy green leaves	slow growing; large bright red berries in autumn
★*Juniperus communis* 'Hibernica' Z 3	small; very columnar	plant in well-drained soil in sun	small resinous-scented prickly blue-green needles with silvery undersides	quick growing; may need tying in as it ages. A good substitute for columnar cypresses in colder areas
★*J. horizontalis* 'Glauca' Z 3	small; ground hugging	plant in well-drained soil in sun or half shade	resinous-scented glaucous steel-blue needles on whipcordlike branches	quick growing; could even be used as a substitute lawn
Laburnum × *watereri* Z 5	small; rounded dome	as above	drooping pea-shaped flower spikes in early summer. Oval shiny green leaves with paler hairy undersides	poisonous seeds in shiny seed pods
Larix decidua 'Fastigiata' Z 2	large; lozenge-shaped	as above	resinous-scented bright green needles in tufts, turning golden in autumn	quick growing
★*Laurus nobilis* Z 8	small; bushy	as above	inconspicuous yellow-green flowers in spring. Thick oval green leaves with wavy edges are highly fragrant when crushed	slow growing
‡★*Ligustrum vulgare* Z 5	small; bushy	plant in well-drained soil in any situation	strongly scented dull white flowers in midsummer. Small narrowly oval shiny dark green leaves	often used as hedging plant; small black fruits; both evergreen and semievergreen
Liquidamber styraciflua Z 5	large; rounded	plant in acidic soil in sun or half-shade	inconspicuous flowers. Five- to seven-lobed toothed shiny green leaves turning crimson in autumn	corky bark of older twigs often a feature in winter
Liriodendron tulipifera Z 4	large; rounded	plant in well-drained soil in sun or half-shade	large tulip-shaped yellow-green flowers with orange inside cups in midspring. Large four-lobed green leaves turning rich butter-yellow in autumn	quick growing; may take twenty years to flower

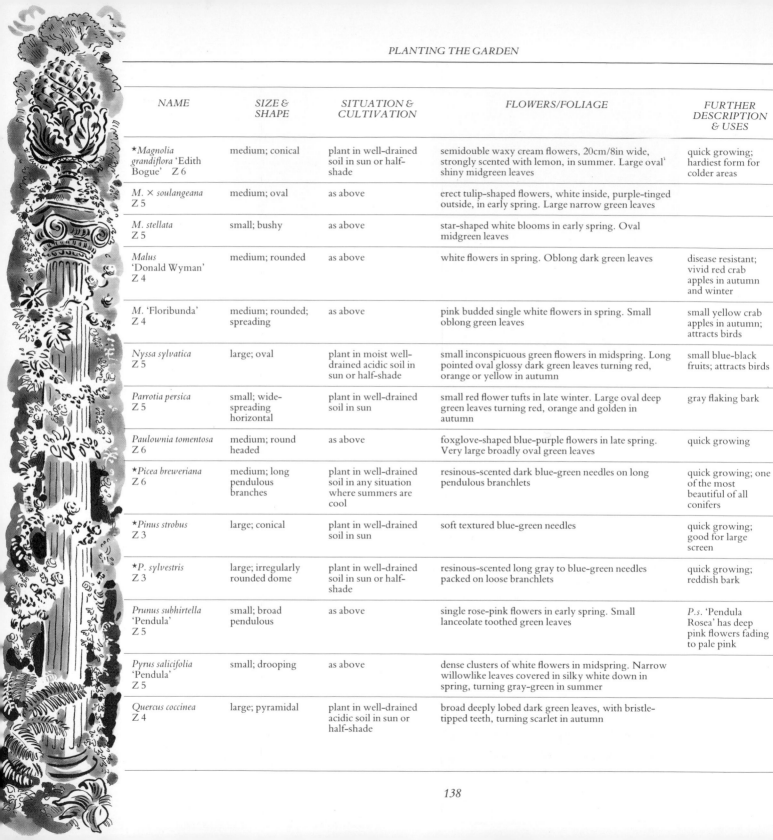

NAME	SIZE & SHAPE	SITUATION & CULTIVATION	FLOWERS/FOLIAGE	FURTHER DESCRIPTION & USES
★*Magnolia grandiflora* 'Edith Bogue' Z 6	medium; conical	plant in well-drained soil in sun or half-shade	semidouble waxy cream flowers, 20cm/8in wide, strongly scented with lemon, in summer. Large oval' shiny midgreen leaves	quick growing; hardiest form for colder areas
M. × *soulangeana* Z 5	medium; oval	as above	erect tulip-shaped flowers, white inside, purple-tinged outside, in early spring. Large narrow green leaves	
M. stellata Z 5	small; bushy	as above	star-shaped white blooms in early spring. Oval midgreen leaves	
Malus 'Donald Wyman' Z 4	medium; rounded	as above	white flowers in spring. Oblong dark green leaves	disease resistant; vivid red crab apples in autumn and winter
M. 'Floribunda' Z 4	medium; rounded; spreading	as above	pink budded single white flowers in spring. Small oblong green leaves	small yellow crab apples in autumn; attracts birds
Nyssa sylvatica Z 5	large; oval	plant in moist well-drained acidic soil in sun or half-shade	small inconspicuous green flowers in midspring. Long pointed oval glossy dark green leaves turning red, orange or yellow in autumn	small blue-black fruits; attracts birds
Parrotia persica Z 5	small; wide-spreading horizontal	plant in well-drained soil in sun	small red flower tufts in late winter. Large oval deep green leaves turning red, orange and golden in autumn	gray flaking bark
Paulownia tomentosa Z 6	medium; round headed	as above	foxglove-shaped blue-purple flowers in late spring. Very large broadly oval green leaves	quick growing
★*Picea breweriana* Z 6	medium; long pendulous branches	plant in well-drained soil in any situation where summers are cool	resinous-scented dark blue-green needles on long pendulous branchlets	quick growing; one of the most beautiful of all conifers
★*Pinus strobus* Z 3	large; conical	plant in well-drained soil in sun	soft textured blue-green needles	quick growing; good for large screen
★*P. sylvestris* Z 3	large; irregularly rounded dome	plant in well-drained soil in sun or half-shade	resinous-scented long gray to blue-green needles packed on loose branchlets	quick growing; reddish bark
Prunus subhirtella 'Pendula' Z 5	small; broad pendulous	as above	single rose-pink flowers in early spring. Small lanceolate toothed green leaves	*P.s.* 'Pendula Rosea' has deep pink flowers fading to pale pink
Pyrus salicifolia 'Pendula' Z 5	small; drooping	as above	dense clusters of white flowers in midspring. Narrow willowlike leaves covered in silky white down in spring, turning gray-green in summer	
Quercus coccinea Z 4	large; pyramidal	plant in well-drained acidic soil in sun or half-shade	broad deeply lobed dark green leaves, with bristle-tipped teeth, turning scarlet in autumn	

NAME	SIZE & SHAPE	SITUATION & CULTIVATION	FLOWERS/FOLIAGE	FURTHER DESCRIPTION & USES
Q. robur Z 5	large; rounded	plant in well-drained soil in sun or half-shade	oblong multilobed dark green leaves, with paler undersides, turning orange to rust-brown in autumn	one to several fruits (acorns) on a stalk
Robinia pseudoacacia Z 4	large; rounded dome, irregular with age	plant in well-drained soil in sun	fragrant clusters of pea-shaped white flowers in early summer. Large pinnate green leaves	fast growing
Salix babylonica Z 6	medium; drooping	plant in moist well-drained soil in sun or half-shade	catkins in late winter and early spring. Long narrow green leaves with blue-green undersides	invasive; becomes brittle with age
S. matsudana 'Tortuosa' Z 4	medium; much twisted branches	plant in well-drained soil in sun or half-shade	yellow catkins in spring. Slender pointed green leaves with glaucous undersides	slow growing
Sophora japonica 'Pendula' Z 4	small; drooping	plant in well-drained soil in any situation	pea-shaped cream-white flowers in late summer and autumn. Green pinnate leaves	seldom flowers
Sorbus alnifolia Z 5	small; round headed	plant in well-drained soil in sun or half-shade	clusters of small white flowers in late spring. Oval dense leaves turning orange and yellow in autumn	orange-red fruit in autumn and winter
Stewartia sinensis Z 6	small; upright	plant in moist well-drained acidic soil in half-shade	fragrant cup-shaped single white or cream flowers in leaf axils in mid- to late summer. Oval green leaves turning rich golden in autumn	attractive flaking bark
Syringa vulgaris Z 3	small; rounded	plant in well-drained soil in sun	fragrant multifloret white, pink, mauve and purple flower heads in spring and early summer. Pointed oval green leaves	many cultivars available
Taxodium distichum Z 5	large; lozenge-shaped	plant in moist acidic soil in sun or half-shade	fresh green needles on red stemmed branchlets turning bronze in autumn	quick growing; half-hardy; striking red-brown bark
Tilia petiolaris Z 6	large; round headed, drooping branches	plant in well-drained soil in any situation	fragrant small cream-white flowers in midsummer. Broadly oval sharp-toothed dark green leaves with white felted undersides	flowers are narcotic to bees!
Zelkova serrata Z 5	large; rounded	plant in moist well-drained soil in shade or half-shade	small inconspicuous green flowers in spring. Long oval pointed coarse-toothed green leaves turning bronze-red in autumn	gray flaking bark

—SHRUBS—

NAME	SIZE & SHAPE	SITUATION & CULTIVATION	FLOWERS/FOLIAGE	FURTHER DESCRIPTION & USES
Acer palmatum 'Dissectum' Z 6	large; round, bushy; slow growing	plant in well-drained soil in half-shade	finely cut fresh green leaves turn bronze-yellow in autumn	
Amelanchier canadensis Z 4	large; erect, twiggy; quick growing	plant in moist well-drained acidic soil in sun or half-shade	small white flower clusters in spring. Pink to copper colored leaves in spring turn red and yellow in autumn	valuable spring and autumn display

NAME	SIZE & SHAPE	SITUATION & CULTIVATION	FLOWERS/FOLIAGE	FURTHER DESCRIPTION & USES
Aralia elata Z 3	large; erect, arching – can become multi-stemmed; quick growing	plant in well-drained soil in any situation	panicles of white flowers in early autumn. Very large light green compound leaves	grown for its dramatic form; may be invasive in some areas
★*Arundinaria murielae* Z 7	large; arching clumps; quick growing	plant in well-drained soil in any situation in a sheltered site	bright green leaves, which yellow as they age	noninvasive
★*A. nitida* Z 6	large; tall arching clumps; quick growing	as above	lush green leaves striped with purple	
Buddleia alternifolia Z 6	large; elegant arching fronds; quick growing	plant in dry well-drained soil in sun or half-shade	massed tiny purple florets in early summer. Thin willowlike green leaves	thin stems crusted with blooms
★*Buxus sempervirens* 'Pendula' Z 5	medium; mound-like; medium growing	plant in well-drained soil in sun	no floral display; shiny evergreen foliage	can be trained as a small tree
★*Cailicarpa bodinieri* var *giraldii* Z 5	large; erect; quick growing	plant in well-drained soil in sun or half-shade	insignificant lilac flowers in summer. Oval midgreen leaves	grown for spectacular pale purple clusters of berries in autumn
★*Camellia japonica* Z 7	large; shrubby; quick growing	plant in well-drained acidic soil in shade or half-shade	forms with red, pink or white flowers with yellow stamens in spring; sometimes marbled white flowers. Glossy dark green leaves	best in protected location
Caryopteris ×clandonensis Z 5	small; forms low mound of arching branches; medium growing	plant in well-drained soil in sun	massed bright blue florets in late summer to autumn. Fragrant oval thin gray-green foliage	prune hard in late winter
Chaenomeles japonica Z 5 .	small; bushy; medium growing	plant in well-drained soil in sun or half-shade	saucer-shaped bright orange flowers in early spring. Small oval green leaves	
Chimonanthus praecox Z 6	large; erect, loose, bushy; medium growing	plant in moist well-drained soil in sun or half-shade	exceedingly fragrant sweet-smelling small pale yellow flowers with purple centers in winter on leafless branches. Oval midgreen leaves	
Clerodendrum trichotomum Z 6	large; erect; quick growing	as above	clusters of fragrant star-shaped white flowers in mid- to late summer. Oval pointed shiny midgreen leaves with unpleasant smell if crushed	prominent bright blue fruits in autumn subtended by a prominent red calyx
Cornus alba var. *sibirica* Z 2	large; wide spreading	plant in well-drained soil in sun or half-shade	oval opposite green leaves	attractive young crimson shoots in winter
Corylus avellana 'Contorta' Z 5	large; curiously twisted branches; slow growing	plant in well-drained soil in sun or half-shade	prominent catkins in late winter. Small green leaves	edible nuts in autumn

NAME	SIZE & SHAPE	SITUATION & CULTIVATION	FLOWERS/FOLIAGE	FURTHER DESCRIPTION & USES
‡*Cytisus* × *kewensis* Z 6	small; semi-arching, semi-prostrate; quick growing	plant in well-drained soil in sun	pea-shaped cream flowers in late spring and early summer. Thin dark green leaves	both deciduous and semievergreen
C. × *praecox* Z 6	small; forms mound of arching stems; quick growing	plant in well-drained soil in sun or half-shade	clusters of pungent pea-shaped cream flowers in spring. Small pale green leaves divided into three leaflets	site away from house to avoid unpleasant odor from flowers
Daphne mezereum Z 6	small; erect; slow growing	plant in moist well-drained soil in sun or half-shade	highly fragrant star-shaped mauve flowers in late winter. Small broad lanceolate leathery glossy fresh green leaves	one of the best shrubs to perfume the winter garden
Deutzia gracilis Z 4	large; upright and arching; medium growing	plant in well-drained soil in sun or half-shade	clusters of single pure white flowers in late spring. Thin oval midgreen leaves	prune after flowering
Exochorda racemosa Z 4	large; loose and open; quick growing	plant in well-drained acidic soil in sun or half-shade	clusters of single white flowers with dark eyes in late spring. Oval midgreen leaves	worth planting for its exceptional spring blossom
★*Fatsia japonica* Z 8	medium to large; loose and erect; quick growing	plant in well-drained soil in sun or half-shade	Broad leathery lobed midgreen leaves	half-hardy
Fuchsia magellanica Z 6	medium; bushy; quick growing	plant in well-drained soil in any situation	long slender flower with scarlet tube and violet petals in summer and autumn. Oval green leaves in whorls of three	may die back in cold areas each winter
Hamamelis mollis Z 5	large; open habit; medium growing	plant in moist well-drained soil in sun or half-shade	small clusters of fragrant yellow flowers in late winter. Broad toothed pointed midgreen leaves with downy undersides	good for forcing cut branches indoors
Hibiscus syriacus 'Diane' Z 5	large; compact; quick growing	plant in well-drained soil in sun	large open trumpet-shaped white flowers from mid- to late summer and early autumn. Circular toothed midgreen leaves	can be pruned hard in spring
Hydrangea macrophylla 'Blue Wave' Z 6	medium; erect; quick growing	plant in well-drained acidic soil in shade or half-shade	large clusters of blue florets surrounded by sterile showy outer florets in late summer and autumn. Oval toothed pointed bright green leaves	many different cultivars available
H. sargentiana Z 6	large; erect; quick growing	as above	large clusters of blue florets surrounded by white outer florets in late summer and autumn. Very large oval pointed velvet-green leaves on woolly stems	prefers a sheltered site
★*Hypericum calycinum* Z 5	small; spreading mound; quick growing	plant in dry well-drained soil in any situation	large cup-shaped yellow flowers in summer and autumn. Oval fresh green leaves	excellent ground cover
Jasminum nudiflorum Z 6	large; loose trailing; quick growing	plant in well-drained soil in sun or half-shade	small trumpet-shaped bright yellow flowers in late autumn and winter on bare stems. Narrow shiny midgreen leaves	also makes an excellent climber and trailer
★*Juniperus squamata* 'Blue Star' Z 4	small; spreading; slow growing	as above	very dense steel-blue needles	tolerant of heat and drought

NAME	SIZE & SHAPE	SITUATION & CULTIVATION	FLOWERS/FOLIAGE	FURTHER DESCRIPTION & USES
★*Kalmia latifolia* Z 4	large; bushy	plant in well-drained acidic soil in shade or half-shade	clusters of saucer-shaped bright pink flowers in summer. Large oval glossy evergreen leaves	many different cultivars available
Kolkwitzia amabilis Z 4	large; dense bushy; medium growing	plant in well-drained soil in sun	small bell-shaped pink flowers in late spring. Small oval pointed hairy leaves	attractive scaling brown bark in winter
Magnolia virginiana Z 5	large; erect, open; medium growing	plant in acidic soil in sun or half-shade; tolerant of wet situations	small fragrant cream-white flowers in early summer. Long oval glossy green leaves with white undersides	adapted to training as wall plant
★*Mahonia bealei* Z 6	medium; erect; medium growing	plant in well-drained soil in shade or half-shade	fragrant clusters of cup-shaped lemon-yellow flowers in late winter. Pinnate dark green leaves with oval prickly edged leaflets	attractive blue fruits
★*Osmanthus heterophyllus* Z 7	small; spreading, rounded, bushy; medium growing	plant in well-drained soil in half-shade	highly fragrant small tubular white flowers in early autumn. Small oval toothed leathery evergreen leaves	
‡*Paeonia suffruticosa* Z 5	large; loose and open; quick growing	plant in well-drained soil in sun or half-shade	large cup-shaped flesh pink flowers with silver-white and maroon splashed at base of petals in early summer. Green leaves	numerous cultivars offer flowers ranging from white through to bright red
Perovskia atriplicifolia 'Blue Spire' Z 7	small; bushy; quick growing	plant in well-drained soil in sun	fragrant narrow panicles of lavender-blue flowers in late summer. Deeply cut gray-green leaves	
Philadelphus × *virginalis* 'Virginal' Z 4	large; erect, bushy; quick growing	plant in well-drained soil in sun or half-shade	extremely fragrant double cup-shaped white flowers in late spring. Oval pointed midgreen leaves	
★*Pieris* 'Forest Flame' Z 6	large; erect, dense, bushy; medium growing	plant in well-drained acidic soil in shade or half-shade	large drooping panicles of urn-shaped white flowers in late spring. Oval lanceolate toothed glossy leaves which when young are red and gradually turn through pink and cream-white to dark green	excellent hedging
Potentilla fruticosa 'Veitchii' Z 2	small; rounded; medium growing	plant in well-drained soil in sun or half-shade	single cup-shaped delicate white flowers with yellow eyes from summer until first frosts. Small pinnate bright green leaves with oval leaflets	many different cultivars available
★*Rhododendron* 'Boule de Neige' Z 6	large; erect; medium growing	plant in well-drained acidic soil in half-shade	large clusters of long bell-shaped white flowers from late spring to early summer. Oblong prominently veined lustrous evergreen leaves	one of the best white-flowered varieties
★*R.* 'PJM' Z 4	medium; erect; medium growing	as above	clusters of lavender-pink flowers in early spring. Small oval green leaves turning wine color in autumn	one of the hardiest evergreen rhododendrons

142

NAME	SIZE	SITUATION & CULTIVATION	FLOWERS/FOLIAGE	FURTHER DESCRIPTION & USES
R. prunifolium Z 6	large; erect; medium growing	plant in well-drained acidic soil in half-shade	clusters of tubular orange-red flowers in late summer. Oval glossy green leaves turning yellow in autumn	
Rhus typhina 'Laciniata' Z 3	large; loose and open; quick growing	plant in well-drained soil in sun or half-shade	insignificant greenish-white flowers in midspring. Large pinnate green leaves with lanceolate toothed leaflets turning orange and red in autumn	crimson fruit spikes only on female plant
Salix caprea Z 4	large; rounded; quick growing	plant in moist well-drained soil in half-shade	yellow male catkins and silver female catkins in early spring. Oval green leaves with gray undersides	
Spirea nipponica 'Snow Mound' Z 4	small; erect; quick growing	plant in well-drained soil in sun	clusters of small white flowers in spring. Narrow fresh green leaves	
S. × bumalda 'Anthony Waterer' Z 5	small; bushy; quick growing	as above	carmine-pink flowers forming flat heads from mid-summer to autumn. Lanceolate toothed cream-tipped and pink-edged leaves when young turning mid-green	*S.b.* 'Gold Flame' has crimson flowers. Bright gold young foliage turning soft yellow
⋆*Viburnum × burkwoodii* Z 5	medium; erect; quick growing	plant in well-drained soil in shade or half-shade	clusters of fragrant white flowers in early spring. Oval shiny green leaves with brownish-gray undersides	
V. carlesii Z 4	medium; rounded; quick growing	plant in well-drained soil in half-shade	rounded clusters of pure white flowers, with sweet daphnelike scent, in spring. Downy dull green leaves with gray undersides turning wine-red in autumn	pink buds; jet black fruit in autumn
⋆*V. plicatum* var. *tormentosum* Z 4	large; dense; quick growing	plant in well-drained soil in any situation	'lace cap' clusters of white flowers in spring. Oval dull green leaves	red fruits turning to black in midsummer
⋆*Yucca filamentosa* Z 4	large; very erect; quick growing	as above	erect panicles of large drooping bell-shaped cream-white flowers in early summer. Large spiky rosettes of long narrow pointed shiny midgreen leaves	splendidly architectural plant; drought tolerant

—CLIMBERS & WALL PLANTS—

NAME	SIZE	SITUATION & CULTIVATION	FLOWERS/FOLIAGE	FURTHER DESCRIPTION & USES
Actinidia arguta Z 4	large	plant in well-drained soil in sun	clusters of cup-shaped cream flowers in later summer. Oval prominently veined dark green leaves	both male and female plants are necessary to produce (edible) fruit
A. kolomikta Z 4	small	as above	cup-shaped cream flowers turn buff-yellow during late summer. Heart-shaped green leaves turn cream and pink variegated	grown as much for its notable foliage as for its flowers
‡*Akebia quinata* Z 5	large	plant in well-drained soil in any situation	fragrant red and purple racemes in spring. Each leaf comprises five notched leaflets	grown primarily for its foliage

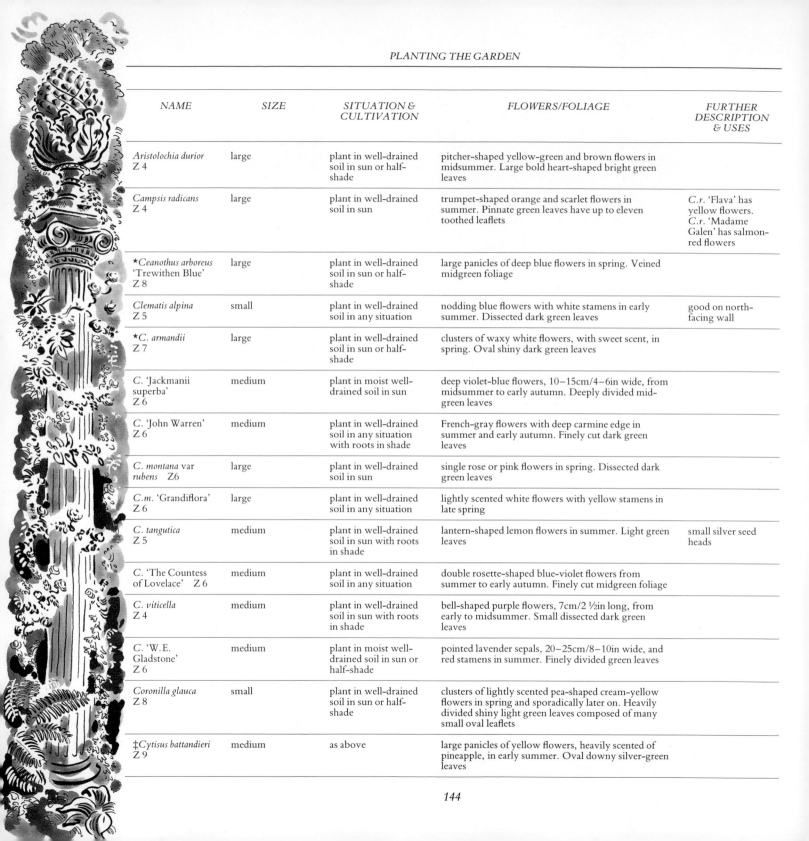

NAME	SIZE	SITUATION & CULTIVATION	FLOWERS/FOLIAGE	FURTHER DESCRIPTION & USES
Aristolochia durior Z 4	large	plant in well-drained soil in sun or half-shade	pitcher-shaped yellow-green and brown flowers in midsummer. Large bold heart-shaped bright green leaves	
Campsis radicans Z 4	large	plant in well-drained soil in sun	trumpet-shaped orange and scarlet flowers in summer. Pinnate green leaves have up to eleven toothed leaflets	*C.r.* 'Flava' has yellow flowers. *C.r.* 'Madame Galen' has salmon-red flowers
★*Ceanothus arboreus* 'Trewithen Blue' Z 8	large	plant in well-drained soil in sun or half-shade	large panicles of deep blue flowers in spring. Veined midgreen foliage	
Clematis alpina Z 5	small	plant in well-drained soil in any situation	nodding blue flowers with white stamens in early summer. Dissected dark green leaves	good on north-facing wall
★*C. armandii* Z 7	large	plant in well-drained soil in sun or half-shade	clusters of waxy white flowers, with sweet scent, in spring. Oval shiny dark green leaves	
C. 'Jackmanii superba' Z 6	medium	plant in moist well-drained soil in sun	deep violet-blue flowers, 10–15cm/4–6in wide, from midsummer to early autumn. Deeply divided mid-green leaves	
C. 'John Warren' Z 6	medium	plant in well-drained soil in any situation with roots in shade	French-gray flowers with deep carmine edge in summer and early autumn. Finely cut dark green leaves	
C. montana var *rubens* Z6	large	plant in well-drained soil in sun	single rose or pink flowers in spring. Dissected dark green leaves	
C.m. 'Grandiflora' Z 6	large	plant in well-drained soil in any situation	lightly scented white flowers with yellow stamens in late spring	
C. tangutica Z 5	medium	plant in well-drained soil in sun with roots in shade	lantern-shaped lemon flowers in summer. Light green leaves	small silver seed heads
C. 'The Countess of Lovelace' Z 6	medium	plant in well-drained soil in any situation	double rosette-shaped blue-violet flowers from summer to early autumn. Finely cut midgreen foliage	
C. viticella Z 4	medium	plant in well-drained soil in sun with roots in shade	bell-shaped purple flowers, 7cm/2 ½in long, from early to midsummer. Small dissected dark green leaves	
C. 'W.E. Gladstone' Z 6	medium	plant in moist well-drained soil in sun or half-shade	pointed lavender sepals, 20–25cm/8–10in wide, and red stamens in summer. Finely divided green leaves	
Coronilla glauca Z 8	small	plant in well-drained soil in sun or half-shade	clusters of lightly scented pea-shaped cream-yellow flowers in spring and sporadically later on. Heavily divided shiny light green leaves composed of many small oval leaflets	
‡*Cytisus battandieri* Z 9	medium	as above	large panicles of yellow flowers, heavily scented of pineapple, in early summer. Oval downy silver-green leaves	

NAME	SIZE	SITUATION & CULTIVATION	FLOWERS/FOLIAGE	FURTHER DESCRIPTION & USES
★*Fremontodendron californicum* 'Californian Glory' Z 9	large	plant in well-drained soil in sun	single cup-shaped golden-yellow flowers throughout summer. Palmate dark green leaves with a rich brown felt	
★*Hedera canariensis* Z 8	large	plant in well-drained soil in shade or half-shade	small green umbels in late summer. Broad five- to seven-lobed light matt green leaves	
★*H. colchica* Z 7	large	plant in dry well-drained soil in shade or half-shade	small green umbels in summer. Very large ovate thick leathery dark green leaves	
★*H. helix* Z 6	large	plant in well-drained soil in shade or half-shade	small green umbels in autumn. Three- or five-lobed dark green leaves	black fruit, also makes excellent ground cover. *H.h.* 'Baltica' hardier. (Z 5)
Hydrangea anomala ssp *petiolaris* Z 5	large	plant in well-drained acidic soil in sun or half-shade	large flat-topped green-white racemes with marginal white florets in early summer. Oval pointed bright green leaves	clings with its aerial rootlets
Jasminum officinale Z 7	large	plant in well-drained soil in sun or half-shade	highly fragrant clusters of small trumpet-shaped white flowers from late spring to autumn. Pinnate dark green leaves of five to nine small lanceolate leaflets	
Lonicera × americana Z 5	large	plant in well-drained soil in any situation	fragrant clusters of white flowers, turning deep yellow, in early summer. Broadly elliptical bright green leaves	purple tinted buds; excellent climbing through trees and hedges as well as on walls
★*L. japonica* 'Aureo-reticulata' Z 5	large	plant in well-drained soil in any situation	insignificant flowers in summer and early autumn. Broadly elliptical bright green leaves with prominent gold veins	
‡*L. japonica* 'Halliana' Z 4	large	plant in well-drained soil in sun or half-shade	highly fragrant clusters of white flowers, turning yellow, in late spring. Oval bright green leaves	can be invasive in some areas
L. periclymenum 'Serotina' Z 5	medium	as above	highly fragrant clusters of trumpet-shaped rich red-purple flowers, yellow within, from early summer to early autumn. Oval midgreen leaves	attractive red berries in autumn
Parthenocissus henryana Z 6	medium	plant in well-drained soil in any situation	three- or five-lobed dark velvet-green leaves, with pink and silver veins, turning bright red in autumn	
P. quinquefolia Z 4	large	plant in well-drained soil in sun or half-shade	five oval stalked dull green leaflets, with shiny undersides, turning orange to scarlet in autumn	self-clinging; small blue-black fruit
Passiflora caerulea Z 9	medium	plant in well-drained soil in sun	highly scented star-shaped white and purple flowers with conspicuous centers in summer and early autumn. Palmate five- to seven-lobed dark green leaves	after a hot summer will produce oval orange edible fruits

NAME	SIZE & SHAPE	SITUATION & CULTIVATION	FLOWERS/FOLIAGE	FURTHER DESCRIPTION & USES
Polygonum aubertii Z 4	large	plant in well-drained soil in sun or half-shade	thick panicles of cream flowers faintly tinted pink from high summer to autumn. Medium to large pale green leaves	quick growing; tolerates poor conditions
★*Trachelospermum jasminoides* Z 9	large	as above	very sweet-scented tiny trumpet-shaped white flowers in late summer. Long oval very shiny dark green leaves	
Tropaeolum speciosum Z9	small	as above	trumpet-shaped bright scarlet flowers in summer. Circular green leaves	
Vitis coignetiae Z 5	large	as above	extremely sweet-scented clusters of small cream flowers in early summer. Enormous wide circular shallowly lobed green leaves, with light undersides, turning crimson and scarlet in autumn	
Vitis vinifera 'Brant' Z 6	large	plant in well-drained soil in sun or half-shade	small light green flowers in summer. Large three- to five-lobed green leaves turning crimson, orange and pink in autumn	edible sweet purple-black grapes in autumn
Wisteria floribunda 'Macrobotrys' Z 5	large	plant in well-drained soil in sun	fragrant racemes of lilac flowers, over 30cm/12in long – sometimes as much as 0.9m/3ft – tinged with blue-purple in spring. Pinnate light green leaves	
W. sinensis Z 5	large	as above	long racemes of fragrant pea-shaped mauve or deep violet flowers in spring. Light green leaves with up to thirteen elliptical leaflets	*W.s.* 'Alba' has white flowers and is powerfully scented

— ROSES —

NAME	SIZE & SHAPE	SITUATION & CULTIVATION	FLOWERS/FOLIAGE	FURTHER DESCRIPTION & USES
Rosa 'Betty Prior' Z 4	H 1.2m/4ft; dense	plant in moist well-drained soil in sun	spicy-scented single light pink flowers from late spring until frost. Oval green leaves	heavy bloomer; flowers are a deeper color in cool weather
R. 'Bonica' Z 3	H 1.5m/5ft; dense	as above	slightly fragrant clear pink flowers from late spring until frost. Oval glossy deep green leaves	disease resistant; do not dead-head in late season, to get orange-red hips
R. 'Carefree Beauty' Z 4	H 1.2m/4ft; dense	as above	slightly fragrant clear pink flowers from late spring until frost. Oval glossy dark green leaves	highly disease resistant; orange-red hips in autumn
R. 'Golden Showers' Z 5	H 2.5m/8ft; climber	as above	remontant slightly fragrant bright yellow flowers, 13cm/5in across, in late spring and summer. Oval smooth glossy dark green leaves	good on pillars and walls
R. 'Madame Hardy' Z 4	H 1.8m/6ft; erect	plant in moist well-drained soil in sun or half-shade	strongly scented very double camellialike pure white flowers with greenish center in summer. Oval green foliage	

NAME	SIZE & SHAPE	SITUATION & CULTIVATION	FLOWERS/FOLIAGE	FURTHER DESCRIPTION & USES
R. moyesii 'Geranium' Z 6	H 3m/10ft; erect, arching	plant in moist well-drained soil in sun or half-shade	single scarlet flowers, 5cm/2in wide, with gold stamens in summer. Typical shrub rose foliage	crimson bottle-shaped hips in autumn
R. mundi Z 5	H 1.5m/5ft; bushy	plant in well-drained soil in sun or half-shade	semidouble crimson flowers with splashes of pink and white in summer. Oval green leaves	quick growing shrub rose
R. primula Z 7	H 2m/6ft 6in; erect	plant in moist well-drained soil in sun or half-shade	fragrant single flat pale yellow flowers in late spring. Small lightly aromatic leaves with seven to thirteen green leaflets	
R. rubrifolia Z 2	H 1.8m/6ft; loose, arching	plant in well-drained soil in any situation	small single pink flowers in summer. Oval plum-gray foliage	quick growing; excellent for hedging
R. rugosa Z 2	H 1.5m/5ft; dense, bushy	as above	remontant single wine-crimson flowers in summer. Finely wrinkled leathery glossy apple-green leaves	quick growing; round flattened crab-apple-shaped hips
R.r. 'Alba' Z 2	H 1.8m/6ft; dense, bushy	plant in moist well-drained soil in sun	remontant fragrant single white flowers in late spring and early summer, occasional light flowering until frost. Oval shiny rough-veined dark green leaves	highly disease resistant; round flattened orange-red hips
R.r. 'Blanc Double de Coubert' Z 2	H 1.8m/6ft; arching	plant in well-drained soil in sun or half-shade	remontant strongly fragrant large semidouble pure white flowers in late summer. Small green leaves	
R.r. 'Parfum de L'Hay' Z 4	H 1.8m/6ft; bushy	plant in moist well-drained soil in sun or half-shade	remontant extremely fragrant very double medium-sized crimson flowers in summer. Oval green leaves	possibly the strongest perfumed rose of all
R.r. 'Pink Grootendorst' Z 4	H 0.9m/3ft; erect	plant in well-drained soil in sun or half-shade	remontant large clusters of small loosely double pink flowers in summer. Small wrinkled green leaves on very prickly stems	
R.r. 'Rubra' Z 2	H 1.8m/6ft; dense, bushy	plant in moist well-drained soil in sun	remontant fragrant single magenta-red flowers in late spring and early summer, occasional light flowering until frost. Oval shiny rough-veined dark green leaves	orange-red hips; prune only to remove old wood
R.r. 'Sir Thomas Lipton' Z 2	H 1.8m/6ft; dense, bushy	as above	remontant highly fragrant double white flowers in late spring and early summer, occasional light flowering until frost. Oval shiny rough-veined dark green foliage	tolerates salt spray
R. spinosissima Z 5	H 1.2m/4ft; dense, bushy	plant in well-drained soil in any situation	small cream-white or pink-white flowers in summer. Fernlike green foliage	quick growing; shiny black hips
R. 'The Fairy' Z 5	H 0.9m/3ft; dense, bushy	plant in moist well-drained soil in sun	remontant fragrant clusters of small pink rosettes from spring until frost. Small oval fine-textured green foliage	can be grown as a low flowering hedge
R. villosa 'Duplex' Z 6	H 1.8m/6ft; densely branched shrub	plant in moist well-drained soil in sun or half-shade	large resinous-scented semidouble clear pink flowers in midsummer. Gray-green leaves typical of shrub rose	globular dark red hips, 3cm/1in long

— PERENNIALS —

NAME	SIZE	SITUATION & CULTIVATION	FLOWERS/FOLIAGE	FURTHER DESCRIPTION & USES
Acanthus mollis Z 5	H 90cm/36in	plant in dry well-drained soil in sun or half-shade	purple or white flowers on spikes in summer. Rich glossy green leaves	
Achillea ageratum Z 5	H 20–30cm/8–12in	plant in well-drained soil in sun	large heads of white florets in summer. Filigree-leaved stems	
Aconitum carmichaeli Z 4	H 120cm/48in	plant in well-drained soil in half-shade	pale hooded rich blue flowers in late summer and autumn. Dissected green foliage	provides good late season color
‡*Agapanthus patens* Z 7	H 60–90cm/24–36in	plant in well-drained soil in sun	clear blue flowers cluster at top of stem from midsummer to early autumn. Straplike green foliage	lightly mulch crown in winter
Anaphalis margaritacea Z 3	H 45cm/18in	plant in well-drained soil in half-shade	erect tufts of loose white flower heads in late summer. Lance-shaped silver leaves	flowers good for drying
Anemone japonica 'Kriemhilde' Z 5	H 75–90cm/30–36in	plant in well-drained soil in sun or half-shade	erect clear pink flowers from late summer to autumn. Divided midgreen foliage	
A. pulsatilla Z 5	H 23–38cm/9–15in	plant in dry well-drained soil in sun	cup-shaped mauve-purple flowers in spring; some red shades. Lacy gray foliage	
Aquilegia biedermeier Z 4	H 45cm/18in	as above	erect stems of pink flowers in summer. Dissected light green foliage	*A.* 'McKana' has flowers of mixed colors. H 90cm/36in
A. flabellata 'Nana'	H 30cm/12in	plant in moist well-drained soil in half-shade	nodding lilac-blue and cream flowers in midspring. Glaucous leaves	*A.f.* var *pumila* 'Alba' has milk-white flowers. H 15cm/6in
Arabis caucasica Z 5	H 60cm/24in	plant in well-drained soil in sun	scented white flowers with yellow stamens in late winter to late spring. Silver-gray foliage forms spreading mounds	good in rock walls
‡*Armeria* 'Bees Ruby'	H 45cm/18in	as above	deep pink flowers in summer. Glossy green leaves	
‡*Artemesia absinthum* Z 5	H 90cm/36in	as above	fragrant panicles of little tight yellow globes in summer. Fragrant finely dissected silver-green leaves	herb used to make absinthe
A. lactifolia Z 5	H 120–150cm/48–60in	as above	slightly sweet-smelling cream flowers, 13mm/½in wide, on plumelike terminal panicles in late summer. Pinnate green leaves with the lobes cut and toothed	
A. 'Silver Queen' Z 5	H 90cm/36in	plant in well-drained soil in sun or shade	small yellow flowers in summer. Fragrant divided silver leaves in clumps	
Aruncus sylvester Z 4	H 120cm/48in	plant in moist well-drained soil in half-shade	feathery cream-white flowers in summer. Small feathery green leaflets in clumps	

NAME	SIZE	SITUATION & CULTIVATION	FLOWERS/FOLIAGE	FURTHER DESCRIPTION & USES
Aster sedifolius Z 6	H 90cm/36in	plant in well-drained soil in sun or half-shade	daisylike light blue to mauve flowers in late summer. Small narrow midgreen foliage forming clumps	
Astilbe 'Ostrich Plume' Z 4	H 60–90cm/24–36in	plant in moist soil in half-shade	pendant bright pink flower spikes in early summer. Finely divided green leaves forming clumps	good for massing
Astrantia involucrata	H 75–90cm/30–36in	plant in well-drained soil in shade	shaggy white flowers in summer. Pointed oval mid-green leaves	
A. major var alba Z 4	H 60–90cm/24–36in	plant in well-drained soil in half-shade	cushionlike silver to rose flowers surrounded by rufflike bracts in summer and autumn. Dissected green leaves forming clumps	A.m.a. 'Rosen Symphonie' has rose-tinted flowers
Athyrium filix-femina Z 3	H 60cm/24in	plant in moist well-drained soil in shade or half-shade	tall lacy gently arching green fronds in tufts	
‡Bergenia cordifolia Z 6	H 38cm/15in	plant in well-drained soil in any situation	clusters of drooping lavender-pink flowers on each flower spike in late spring. Large oval shiny green leaves in untidy clumps	quick growing; needs shade in winter
Brunnera macrophylla Z 3	H 45cm/18in	plant in well-drained soil in sun or shade	sprays of small vivid blue flowers in spring and early summer. Wide round green leaves forming mounds	
Campanula barbata var alba Z 4	H 30cm/12in	plant in well-drained soil in sun	small bell-shaped pure white flowers in summer. Small straplike green leaves	
C. carpatica 'Blue' Z 3	H 30–38cm/12–15in	plant in well-drained soil in sun or half-shade	large open bell-shaped blue flowers in summer. Small straplike midgreen leaves	C.c. 'White' has white flowers
Catanache caerulea Z 4	H 60cm/24in	plant in well-drained soil in sun	semidouble blue flowers in summer. Long straplike hairy leaves	
Centaurea montana	H 38cm/15in	plant in dry well-drained soil in sun	pink, violet or purple flowers in early to mid-summer. Oblong arching silver-gray leaves in clumps	
★Cheiranthus 'Bowles Mauve' Z6	H 90cm/36in	plant in dry well-drained soil in sun	racemes of mauve-purple flowers in spring and intermittently throughout year. Narrow gray leaves	
Cimicifuga racemosa Z 3	H 120cm/48in	plant in moist well-drained soil in shade	slightly fragrant long tapering feathery white plumes in mid- to late summer. Small deeply cut toothed green leaves	
Convallaria majalis Z 3	H 23cm/9in	plant in well-drained soil in half shade	sweet-scented racemes of bell-shaped flowers in spring. Long oval midgreen leaves	good ground cover in shade
Cortaderia selloana Z 7	H 280cm/108in	plant in well-drained soil in sun or half-shade	cream-white feathery plumes in summer. Tough grasslike foliage in large clumps	
Cosmea 'Sensation' Z 7	H 90cm/36in	plant in well-drained soil in sun	single white, pink or mauve flowers with yellow centers in summer. Attractive fernlike foliage in loose clumps	lightly mulch in winter for extra protection
Cynara cardunculus	H 120–180cm/48–72in	as above	thistlelike blue-white flowers in summer and early autumn. Divided gray leaves	

NAME	SIZE	SITUATION & CULTIVATION	FLOWERS/FOLIAGE	FURTHER DESCRIPTION & USES
Delphinium × belladonna 'Blue Bees' Z 3	H 90–120cm/26–38in	plant in moist well-drained soil in sun	tall packed open cup-shaped sky-blue flowers on single flower spike in early to midsummer. Deeply dissected midgreen leaves in clumps	*D.× b.* 'Lamartine' has violet-blue flowers. H 120–220cm/48–84in
★*Dianthus* 'Mrs Sinkins' Z 4	H 45cm/18in	plant in well-drained soil in sun or half-shade	fragrant double pink flowers with maroon eye in summer. Long thin silver-gray leaves forming mounds	
D. plumaris 'Old Laced Pinks' Z 3	H 30cm/12in	plant in dry well-drained soil in sun	fragrant frilly double, semidouble and single flowers in all shades of pink in summer. Short fine gray-green leaves forming mats	
Dicentra exima Z 3	H 15–45cm/6–18in	plant in well-drained soil in half-shade	sprays of locket-shaped pendant rose-mauve, pale rose or white flowers in spring and summer. Fernlike tufted green leaves in mounds	
Dodecatheon meadia Z 4	H 38cm/15in	plant in well-drained soil in shade	clusters of rose-purple blooms with reflexed petals and bright yellow anthers in late spring. Long oval green leaves in rosettes	
★*Dryas octopetala* Z 4	H 8–15cm/3–6in	plant in moist well-drained acid soil in sun or half-shade	open cream-white flowers with yellow centers in late spring and early summer. Small oval green leaves forming spreading mats	
Echinops ritro Z 3	H 120–180cm/48–72in	plant in well-drained soil in sun	globe-shaped steel-blue flowers in summer. Much divided spiny blue-gray leaves	
‡*Epimedium grandiflorum* Z 5	H 23cm/9in	plant in well-drained soil in shade	loose sprays of small white, bright yellow, deep red and bright violet flowers in early spring. Glossy green leaves, tinged bronze in autumn, in spreading clumps	good ground cover; tolerant of dry soil
‡*Eriophorum latifolium*	H 60cm/24in	plant in moist well-drained acid soil in sun or half-shade	cottony white tufts on wiry stems in summer. Long thin green leaves in clumps	
Eryngium alpinum Z 5	H 60cm/24in	plant in well-drained soil in sun or half-shade	gun-metal blue feathery flowers with prominent centers in summer. Deeply cut toothed blue-green leaves in clumps	
Euphorbia characias Z 6	H 90–120cm/36–48in	plant in dry well-drained soil in sun or half shade	clusters of yellow-green flowers in early summer. Gray-green foliage	
★*E. robbiae* Z 6	H 90cm/36in	as above	clusters of yellow-green flowers in spring and early summer. Gray-green leaves	
E. wulfenii Z 6	H 90–120cm/36–48in	plant in dry well-drained soil in sun	clusters of bright yellow-green flowers in spring and early summer. Gray-green leaves	
‡*Festuca ovina* var *glauca* Z 4	H 15–20cm/6–8in	plant in well-drained soil in sun or half-shade	purple flowers in panicles in late spring and summer. Long thin silver-blue foliage in dense tufts	tolerant of dry soil
Filipendula ulmaria var *aurea* Z 4	H 60–120cm/24–48in	plant in moist well-drained soil in half-shade	flat clusters of small feathery white flowers in early to midsummer. Large five- or seven-lobed golden-yellow leaves	

NAME	SIZE	SITUATION & CULTIVATION	FLOWERS/FOLIAGE	FURTHER DESCRIPTION & USES
Geranium 'Johnsons Blue' Z 3	H 45cm/18in	plant in well-drained soil in sun	vivid blue flowers in spring to late summer. Divided leaves forming loose mounds	half-hardy
G. pratense Z 4	H 60cm/24in	as above	single soft lavender-blue flowers in summer. Tripennate green leaves forming bushy shape	*G.p.* var *alba* has white flowers
G. 'Russell Prichard' Z 4	H 30–60cm/12–24in	as above	single magenta-pink flowers in summer and early autumn. Soft gray-green leaves forming mounded carpet	
Gypsophila paniculata Z 3	H 90cm/36in	as above	loose delicate sprays of small single white blooms making fluffy clouds in summer.	
Helictotrichon sempervirens Z 5	H 45cm/18in	plant in well-drained soil in sun	silver-blue flower plumes in early summer. Grasslike blue-gray foliage forming hummocks	silver seed heads
Helleborus niger Z 4	H 30cm/12in	plant in well-drained soil in half-shade	large cream-white flowers with golden centers in winter. Oval leathery glossy dark green leaves	best where lightly shaded in winter
‡*Hemerocallis* 'Happy Returns' Z 4	H 45–90cm/18–36in	plant in well-drained soil in sun or half-shade	remontant trumpet-shaped lemon-yellow flowers in summer. Straplike green leaves forming mounds	
× *Heucherella tiarelloides* 'Bridget Bloom' Z 3	H 25–30cm/10–12in	plant in well-drained soil in half-shade	sprays of small white to pink bell-shaped florets in late spring to midsummer and again in early autumn. Small slightly lobed leaves in compact domes	
Hosta fortunei var *aurea* Z 3	H 60–90cm/24–36in	plant in well-drained soil in shade	mauve florets on each stem in summer. Broad pointed green leaves with variegated golden edges	
Iberis sempervirens 'Snowflake' Z 4	H 45–60cm/18–24in	plant in well-drained soil in sun or half-shade	pure white florets forming rounded flower heads in late spring and early summer. Small dark green leaves	best where lightly shaded in winter
‡*Iris kaempferi* Z 5	H 75–90cm/30–36in	plant in moist well-drained soil in sun	large open snow-white, blue or purple flowers in early summer. Erect thin straplike green leaves in clumps	many different cultivars available
I. pallida 'Variegata' Z 4	H 75–90cm/30–36in	plant in well-drained soil in sun	fragrant blue flowers in early summer. Glaucous gray-green swordlike leaves marked with white in fan-shaped clumps	
I. sibirica Z 3	H 90–120cm/36–48in	plant in moist well-drained soil in sun	small blue-white or deep purple flowers in early to midsummer. Swordlike green foliage	many cultivars available
Kniphofia erecta Z 8	H 120cm/48in	plant in dry well-drained soil in sun	poker heads of packed orange-scarlet florets on erect flowering stems in late summer. Swordlike green leaves forming untidy clumps	
Lamium maculatum 'Chequers' Z 4	H 20–23cm/8–9in	plant in moist well-drained soil in shade	hooded white and purple-pink flowers in spring. Heart-shaped green leaves heavily spotted with paler gray-green forming prostrate spreading clumps	
Lavatera 'Rose'	H 150cm/60in	plant in well-drained soil in sun	rose-pink flowers in summer. Soft sage-green leaves	
Leontopodium alpinum Z 5	H 10–15cm/4–6in	plant in dry well-drained soil in sun	star-shaped off-white flowers with yellow centers in summer. Narrow woolly silver-gray leaves	best in cool northern gardens

NAME	SIZE	SITUATION & CULTIVATION	FLOWERS/FOLIAGE	FURTHER DESCRIPTION & USES
Liatris pycnostachya Z 3	H 90–120cm/36–48in	plant in well-drained soil in sun	fluffy rose-purple flower spikes in midsummer. Thin arching green foliage	
Linum perenne 'Blue Saphyr' Z 4	H 15–20cm/6–8in	as above	single sky-blue flowers in summer. Gray-green leaves forming mounds	*L.p.* 'White Diamond' has pure white flowers. H 30cm/12in
★*Lithodora diffusum* 'Heavenly Blue' Z 7	H 15cm/6in	as above	fine star-shaped deep blue flowers in late spring and early summer. Dark green needles forming trailing foliage	
Lychnis coronaria 'Abbotswood Rose' Z 6	H 60–90cm/24–36in	plant in dry well-drained soil in sun	open ball-shaped white flowers in summer. Gray-green leaves forming clumps	*L.c.* 'Alba' also has white flowers
Malva alcea 'Fastigiata' Z 4	H 120cm/48in	plant in well-drained soil in sun or half-shade	soft pink flowers in summer and autumn. Heart-shaped lobed silky soft green leaves	
‡*Mentha pulegium* Z 5	H 10–30cm/4–12in	plant in well-drained soil in sun	small lilac flowers in late summer and autumn. Scented oval dark green leaves	
Milium effusum 'Aureum'	H 30–90cm/12–36in	plant in well-drained soil in shade or half-shade	insignificant flowers in summer. Long thin yellow foliage in grassy clumps	
‡*Miscanthus sinensis* 'Silver Fern' Z 4	H 180cm/72in	plant in dry well-drained soil in sun or half-shade	panicles of white flowers tinged red in late summer and autumn. Tall grasslike arching green leaves with white midriffs in dense clumps	
‡*Nepeta* × *faassenii* Z 4	H 30cm/12in	plant in well-drained soil in sun	spikes of lavender-blue flowers in spring and summer. Fragrant small gray leaves forming spreading clumps	cats love this plant!
Oenothera missouriensis Z 4	H 30–45cm/12–18in	as above	funnel-shaped yellow flowers that open at evening in summer. Small oval green leaves forming mounds	
Paeonia 'Kelways Lovely' Z 3	H 75–105cm/30–42in	plant in well-drained soil in sun or half-shade	large double rose-pink flowers in spring. Narrow green leaves in clumps	
P. lactiflora Z 3	H 60cm/24in	plant in moist well-drained soil in sun or half-shade	strongly scented large white flowers in early summer. Large incised shiny dark green leaves	many different cultivars available
P. officinalis 'Rubra Plena' Z 3	H 60–90cm/24–36in	plant in well-drained soil in sun or half-shade	globe-shaped crimson flowers in late spring. Large lobed dark green foliage	
Papaver orientale 'Goliath' Z 3	H 90cm/36in	plant in well-drained soil in sun	single open bright red flowers in late spring and early summer. Long fernlike hairy green leaves in clumps	pink and white cultivars available
Pennisetum alopecuroides Z 6	H 30–150cm/12–60in	plant in well-drained soil in sun	insignificant flowers in summer. Long thin green, yellow or purple leaves in grasslike clumps	both hardy and half-hardy.
‡*Phlox douglasii* Z 4	H 10cm/4in	plant in well-drained soil in sun	lavender-pink to white flowers in spring. Pinlike dense dark green foliage	both deciduous and semievergreen

NAME	SIZE	SITUATION & CULTIVATION	FLOWERS/FOLIAGE	FURTHER DESCRIPTION & USES
‡*P. paniculata* 'Admiral' Z 3	H 60–90cm/24–36in	plant in well-drained soil in sun	dense clusters of single white florets in mid- to late summer. Small oval green leaves	*P.p.* 'Sandringham' has pink florets
Physalis alkekengi Z 6	H 45cm/18in	as above	insignificant small white flowers in summer. Large oval green leaves	lantern-shaped orange seed pods
Polygonatum commutatum Z 3	H 75cm/30in	plant in moist well-drained soil in shade	multiple drooping white flowers flushed with green on arching stems in spring. Elongated oval green leaves	
Primula auricula Z 5	H 15–25cm/6–10in	plant in moist well-drained soil in any situation	clusters of narrow bell-shaped green flowers with circle of cream toward center in late spring before leaves appear. Large obovate waxy light green leaves	*P.a.* 'Lovebird' has light green petals.
P. denticulata var *alba* Z 5	H 10–30cm/4–12in	plant in well-drained soil in sun or half-shade	white globes of multiple florets in spring. Bright green leaves forming rosettes	apply light mulch in late autumn
P. veris Z 5	H 23cm/9in	as above	clusters of drooping lemon-yellow florets in spring. Light green leaves forming rosettes	
P. vulgaris Z 5	H 10–20cm/4–8in	plant in moist well-drained soil in shade or half-shade	single open buttercup-yellow flowers with golden centers in spring. Puckered light green leaves in rosettes	
Ranunculus gramineus Z 6	H 38cm/15in	plant in well-drained soil in sun	cup-shaped yellow flowers in late spring and early summer. Narrow grasslike glaucous leaves in small clumps	
Salvia × *superba* Z 4	H 90–120cm/36–48in	as above	multifloret violet-purple flower spikes in summer. Fragrant gray-green leaves	drought and heat tolerant
‡*Saxifraga* 'Cloth of Gold' Z 5	H 8–15cm/3–6in	plant in cool moist well-drained soil in half-shade	white flowers in early summer. Golden foliage in hummocks	
Scabiosa caucasica Z 3	H 75cm/30in	plant in well-drained soil in sun	large lavender-blue flowers in early to late summer. Silver-green foliage in loose clumps	
S. graminifolia Z 4	H 25–30cm/10–12in	as above	mauve-blue flowers with yellow centers in summer and early autumn. Grasslike silver leaves	
‡*Sedum cauticola* Z 4	H 10cm/4in	plant in well-drained soil in sun or half-shade	sprays of small crimson florets in late summer. Blue-gray leaves in spreading tufts	
Solidago canadensis 'Golden Thumb' Z 3	H 30cm/12in	plant in well-drained soil in sun	feathery panicles of deep yellow florets in early summer. Elongated golden-green leaves	
‡*Stachys lanata* Z 4	H 50cm/20in	plant in dry well-drained soil in sun or half-shade	pink flowers in summer. Silver felted leaves with low spreading habit	
Thalictrum aquilegifolium Z 5	H 60–90cm/24–36in	plant in well-drained soil in sun or half-shade	fluffy mauve to white flowers in mid- to late summer. Pinnate blue-gray foliage in loose clumps	

NAME	SIZE	SITUATION & CULTIVATION	FLOWERS/FOLIAGE	FURTHER DESCRIPTION & USES
‡*Thymus serphyllum* var *coccineus* Z 6	H 5–10cm/2–4in	plant in well-drained soil in sun or half-shade	clusters of small red flowers in early summer. Fragrant threadlike leaves forming creeping mats	
Tiarella cordifolia Z 4	H 15–30cm/6–12in	plant in well-drained soil in shade or half-shade	foamy white flowers in spring and early summer. Flat golden-green leaves	good woodland ground cover
Tradescantia virginiana 'Osprey' Z 4	H 30–45cm/12–18in	plant in well-drained soil in sun	three-petaled white multiple florets in summer. Straplike untidy glaucous green leaves	
Verbascum hybridum 'Gainsborough' Z 5	H 150cm/60in	as above	closely packed single cup-shaped light yellow blooms on tapering spikes in summer. Silver-gray leaves forming clumps	
Veronica spicata var *incarna* Z 4	H 60cm/24in	as above	masses of violet flowers on dense tapering spikes in summer. Narrow toothed gray leaves in clumps	
Vinca minor 'Bowles Variety' Z 5	H 15–23cm/6–9in	plant in well-drained soil in shade or half-shade	funnel-shaped bright blue flowers in spring and summer. Small ovate shiny dark green leaves with trailing spreading habit	excellent ground cover
Viola odorata 'Queen Charlotte' Z 6	H 8cm/3in	plant in well-drained soil in sun or half-shade	fragrant small open deep blue flowers in spring. Small oval green leaves in small clumps	

— ANNUALS & BIENNIALS —

NAME	SIZE	SITUATION & CULTIVATION	FLOWERS/FOLIAGE	FURTHER DESCRIPTION & USES
Alcea rosea var *nigra*	H 150cm/60in	plant in well-drained soil in sun	chocolate-maroon flowers, black toward center, in summer. Rough toothed heart-shaped light green leaves	can be grown as an annual or biennial
Alyssum 'Sweet White'	H 8–10cm/3–4in	plant in well-drained soil in sun or half-shade	fragrant small white flowers from early summer to early autumn. Short straplike leaves forming spreading mound	
Antirrhinum 'Lavender Monarch'	H 36–40cm/14–16in	as above	mauve-pink multiflowered spikes from early summer until frosts. Small dark green leaves on flower stem	dead-head for repeat blooming
‡*Briza minor*	H 45cm/18in	as above	shimmering panicles of flowers in summer. Long narrow grassy leaves	graceful pendant seed heads.
Campanula medium 'Bells of Holland'	H 38cm/15in	plant in well-drained soil in sun	large bell-shaped blue, mauve, rose or white flowers in early summer. Small straplike green leaves	biennial
‡*Cineraria maritima*	H 15–20cm/6–8in	plant in well-drained soil in half-shade	neat fernlike woolly silver-gray foliage	can be grown as annual or biennial
Dianthus caryophyllus	H 45–90cm/18–36in	plant in dry well-drained soil in sun	pink carnation flowers, strongly clove scented, in summer. Narrow waxy gray leaves in clumps	biennial or short lived perennial-

NAME	SIZE	SITUATION & CULTIVATION	FLOWERS/FOLIAGE	FURTHER DESCRIPTION & USES
Digitalis purpurea	H 150cm/60in	plant in well-drained soil in sun or half-shade	massed hanging bell-shaped bright pink flowers, with mottled insides, on long erect spikes in summer. Oval soft gray-green leaves	biennial. *D.p.* var *alba* has pure white flowers. H 120cm/48in. *D.p.* 'Apricot' has apricot flowers
Impatiens 'Futura Wild Rose'	H 20–30cm/8–12in	plant in well-drained soil in shade or half-shade	small iridescent cerise flowers throughout summer. Small oval leaves	quick growing. *I.* 'Futura White' has single white flowers. *I.* 'Super Elfin White' has bright white flowers
Ipomoea 'Heavenly Blue'	H 500cm/200in	plant in well-drained soil in sun	large clear blue flowers in summer. Slender pointed ivy-leaf green leaves	vigorous climber
I. purpurea	H 500cm/200in	plant in well-drained soil in sun or half-shade	flowers in shades of white, pink, blue and mauve in summer. Triangular green foliage	quick growing; flowers open only in the morning
Lathyrus odoratus 'Aerospace'	H 150–180cm/60–72in	plant in well-drained soil in sun	fragrant large white flowers in summer. Oval light green leaves	quick growing climber. *L.o.* 'Marietta' has rose-mauve flowers
Lavatera trimestris 'Loveliness'	H 90–120cm/36–48in	as above	large trumpet-shaped rose-pink blooms in summer. Soft light green foliage forming open bush	*L.t.* 'Mont Blanc' has prominent open cups with strongly veined white petals and large leaves.
Lobelia 'Blue Basket'	H 10–15cm/4–6in	plant in well-drained soil in sun or half-shade	violet-blue flowers with white eyes throughout summer. Small narrow lance-shaped toothed green leaves	half-hardy
Lunaria annua var *alba*	H 75cm/30in	plant in well-drained soil in shade or half-shade	clusters of white flowers in late summer. Small pointed oval leaves	biennial; silver seed pods *L.a.* 'Munstead Purple' has velvet-purple flowers
Lupinus argenteus	H 60cm/24in	plant in well-drained soil in sun or half-shade	well spaced lilac to violet flowers in summer. Silver-gray leaves forming bush	biennial
Malcolmia maritima	H 20cm/8in	plant in well-drained soil in sun	small fragrant flowers in all shades of pink, violet, red, blue and white throughout summer. Small narrow green leaves	
Matthiola bicornis	H 30cm/12in	as above	fragrant single lilac flowers in summer. Long thin midgreen leaves	as above
Myosotis sylvatica	H 30cm/12in	plant in moist well-drained soil in half-shade	small rich blue flowers in early summer. Small lance-shaped green leaves in compact mounds	annual or biennial

NAME	SIZE	SITUATION & CULTIVATION	FLOWERS/FOLIAGE	FURTHER DESCRIPTION & USES
Nemophila menziesii	H 15–30cm/6–12in	plant in dry well-drained soil in sun or half-shade	sky-blue flowers, 3cm/1in long, in early summer. Soft fine dissected green leaves that trail	
Nicotiana alata	H 105–120cm/42–48in	plant in well-drained soil in sun	large fragrant trumpet-shaped white flowers throughout summer. Long egg-shaped light green foliage in loose clumps	
Nigella damascena 'Miss Jekyll'	H 45cm/18in	plant in well-drained soil in sun	semidouble cornflower-blue flowers in summer. Delicate finely cut green foliage in feathery clumps	
Papaver 'Fairy Wings'	H 25–36cm/10–14in	as above	single flower heads of mixed pastel shades of pink, white and gray-blue in summer. Small furry light green leaves in clumps	frequently self-seeds
P. rhoeas	H 60cm/24in	as above	single bowl-shaped scarlet flowers with golden stamens all summer. Midgreen leaves in clumps	
Petunia 'Snowcloud'	H 23–30cm/9–12in	plant in well-drained soil in sun or half-shade	soft petaled pure white flowers all summer. Small oval green leaves in loose clumps	
Salvia farinacea 'White Porcelain'	H 38cm/15in	plant in well-drained soil in sun	multiple florets of silver-white flowers on erect stems throughout summer. Dissected silver-gray leaves	*S.f.* 'Victoria' has rich violet-blue flowers. H 45cm/18in
Senecio maritima 'Silver Dust'	H 20cm/8in	plant in well-drained soil in sun	fernlike silver-white foliage in low mounds	grown for its foliage
Tropaeolum majus var *flore plena* 'Orange Gleam'	H 60cm/24in	plant in well-drained soil in sun or half-shade	fragrant deep orange to mahogany flowers all summer. Circular green leaves in open mounds	quick growing; semitrailing
Viola tricolor 'Baby Lucia'	H 15cm/6in	as above	small deep lavender-blue flowers in summer. Small semiserrated green leaves in loose clumps	often self-seeds
Zinnia 'Envy Double'	H 60cm/24in	as above	dahlialike chartreuse-green flowers in late summer. Oval midgreen leaves in clumps	

— BULBS, CORMS & TUBERS —

Allium cernuum	H 30–36cm/12–14in	plant in well-drained soil in sun	pendulous amethyst to lilac-pink multiflowered umbels in summer. Straplike green leaves	good seed heads. Flowers in second season
A. murrayanum	H 30cm/12in	as above	10cm/4in rich pink multistemmed umbels in summer. Straplike green leaves	flowers in second season
A. pulchellum	H 38–45cm/15–18in	as above	loose bright rose-red or red-purple multiflowered umbels in early summer. Straplike green leaves	as above

NAME	SIZE	SITUATION & CULTIVATION	FLOWERS/FOLIAGE	FURTHER DESCRIPTION & USES
A. ursinum Z 7	H 30cm/12in	plant in well-drained soil in half-shade	multiple white florets on single stem in late spring. Straplike green foliage	
Anemone nemorosa	H 15–23cm/6–9in	plant in well-drained soil in shade or half-shade	usually white flowers in early summer. Midgreen foliage	poisonous
Crocosmia masonorum Z 7	H 60cm/24in	plant in well-drained soil in sun	multiple star-shaped orange to flame florets on single arching stem in summer. Erect swordlike foliage	further north lift and store bulbs in winter
Crocus chrysanthus 'Snow Bunting'	H 15cm/6in	plant in well-drained soil in sun or half-shade	white flowers with faint featherings of indigo, yellow base and deep orange stigmata in spring. Upright narrow green foliage	
Cyclamen coum Z 6–7	H 10–15cm/4–6in	plant in well-drained soil in shade or half-shade	deep crimson, carmine or magenta flowers in mid-winter to spring. Flat round dark green foliage, sometimes with red underside	
C. hederifolium	H 10cm/4in	plant in well-drained soil in shade	small red flowers emerging through leaves in late summer to autumn. Flat dark green leaves in clumps	*C.h.* var *album* has dainty white blooms
C. persicum 'Dwarf Fragrance' Z 8	H 20cm/8in	plant in well-drained soil in shade or half-shade	fragrant 4cm/1½in flowers of scarlet, pink, rose, and white with a red eye in autumn and winter. Glaucous leaves	
C. repandum Z 8	H 15cm/6in	plant in well-drained soil in half-shade	fragrant carmine to soft rose flowers in spring. Marbled foliage in mounds	
Eremurus himalaicus Z 5	H 75–120cm/30–48in	plant in well-drained soil in sun	white flowers in late spring to early summer. Rushlike green leaves	
Erythronium dens-canis Z 3	H 15cm/6in	plant in moist well-drained soil in half-shade	small fragrant lilac, pink or rose flowers in spring. Small green foliage in clumps	
Fritillaria meleagris Z 5	H 25–38cm/10–15in	plant in moist well-drained soil in sun or half-shade	beautiful nodding bell-shaped purple and white checkered flowers in midspring. Rushlike green leaves	
Galanthus nivalis	H 15–30cm/6–12in	plant in well-drained soil in shade or half-shade	drooping bell-shaped single white flowers in late winter to early spring. Narrow green foliage in tussocks	naturalizes easily
Iris chrysographes	H 45–60cm/18–24in	plant in well-drained soil in sun	deep maroon to black flowers in early summer. Erect narrow foliage	
I. danfordiae	H 15cm/6in	plant in well-drained soil in sun or half-shade	lemon-yellow flowers in early spring. Light green spikes of leaf	
I. reticulata	H 15cm/6in	plant in moist well-drained soil in shade	deep mauve flowers with gold markings in mid-winter. Swordlike green leaves	
Lilium auratum 'Lavender Princess'	H 120–150cm/48–60in	plant in well-drained acidic soil in sun or half-shade	fragrant cream-white blooms, 20cm/8in across, flecked with lavender, in summer. Multiple blooms on stem, which also has short thin green leaves	

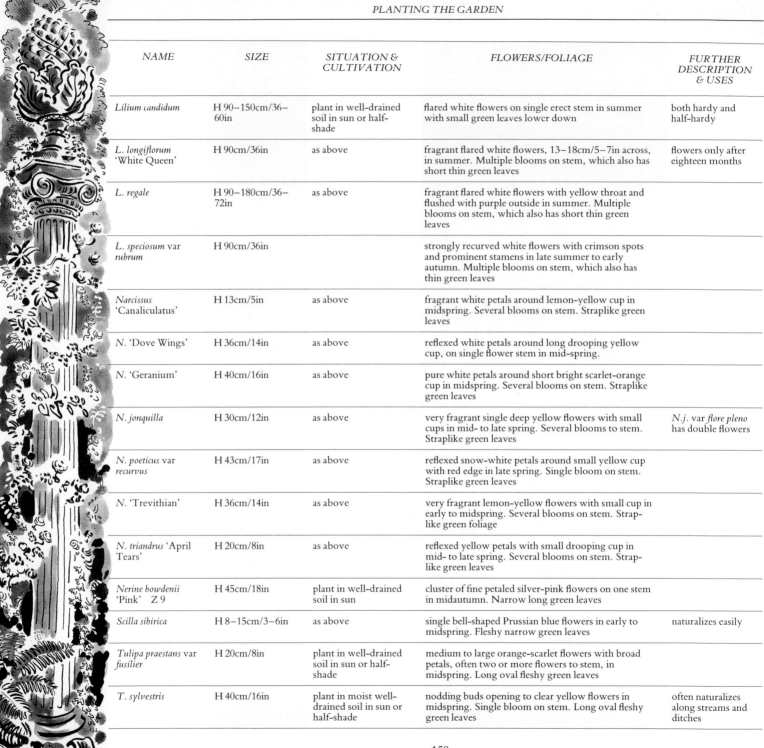

NAME	SIZE	SITUATION & CULTIVATION	FLOWERS/FOLIAGE	FURTHER DESCRIPTION & USES
Lilium candidum	H 90–150cm/36–60in	plant in well-drained soil in sun or half-shade	flared white flowers on single erect stem in summer with small green leaves lower down	both hardy and half-hardy
L. longiflorum 'White Queen'	H 90cm/36in	as above	fragrant flared white flowers, 13–18cm/5–7in across, in summer. Multiple blooms on stem, which also has short thin green leaves	flowers only after eighteen months
L. regale	H 90–180cm/36–72in	as above	fragrant flared white flowers with yellow throat and flushed with purple outside in summer. Multiple blooms on stem, which also has short thin green leaves	
L. speciosum var *rubrum*	H 90cm/36in		strongly recurved white flowers with crimson spots and prominent stamens in late summer to early autumn. Multiple blooms on stem, which also has thin green leaves	
Narcissus 'Canaliculatus'	H 13cm/5in	as above	fragrant white petals around lemon-yellow cup in midspring. Several blooms on stem. Straplike green leaves	
N. 'Dove Wings'	H 36cm/14in	as above	reflexed white petals around long drooping yellow cup, on single flower stem in mid-spring.	
N. 'Geranium'	H 40cm/16in	as above	pure white petals around short bright scarlet-orange cup in midspring. Several blooms on stem. Straplike green leaves	
N. jonquilla	H 30cm/12in	as above	very fragrant single deep yellow flowers with small cups in mid- to late spring. Several blooms to stem. Straplike green leaves	*N.j.* var *flore pleno* has double flowers
N. poeticus var *recurvus*	H 43cm/17in	as above	reflexed snow-white petals around small yellow cup with red edge in late spring. Single bloom on stem. Straplike green leaves	
N. 'Trevithian'	H 36cm/14in	as above	very fragrant lemon-yellow flowers with small cup in early to midspring. Several blooms on stem. Strap-like green foliage	
N. triandrus 'April Tears'	H 20cm/8in	as above	reflexed yellow petals with small drooping cup in mid- to late spring. Several blooms on stem. Strap-like green leaves	
Nerine bowdenii 'Pink' Z 9	H 45cm/18in	plant in well-drained soil in sun	cluster of fine petaled silver-pink flowers on one stem in midautumn. Narrow long green leaves	
Scilla sibirica	H 8–15cm/3–6in	as above	single bell-shaped Prussian blue flowers in early to midspring. Fleshy narrow green leaves	naturalizes easily
Tulipa praestans var *fusilier*	H 20cm/8in	plant in well-drained soil in sun or half-shade	medium to large orange-scarlet flowers with broad petals, often two or more flowers to stem, in midspring. Long oval fleshy green leaves	
T. sylvestris	H 40cm/16in	plant in moist well-drained soil in sun or half-shade	nodding buds opening to clear yellow flowers in midspring. Single bloom on stem. Long oval fleshy green leaves	often naturalizes along streams and ditches

— WATER & WATERSIDE PLANTS —

NAME	SIZE	SITUATION & CULTIVATION	FLOWERS/FOLIAGE	FURTHER DESCRIPTION & USES
Acorus gramineus 'Variegatus' Z 7	H 30cm/12in	plant in wet soil in sun	grasslike variegated green and yellow foliage	
Aponogeton distachyus Z 9	H 30cm/12in	plant in water in sun	fragrant forked white flowers throughout summer. Floating straplike green leaves	
Caltha palustris Z 2	H 38cm/15in	plant in wet soil in shade or half-shade	golden-yellow flowers in early spring to summer. Grasslike leaves in tufts	
Gunnera manicata Z 9	H 3m/10ft	plant in wet soil in shade	rust-brown flower spikes, up to 180cm/6ft long, throughout summer. Very large green leaves	
Iris laevigata Z 4	H 45cm/18in	plant in moist well-drained soil in sun or half-shade	brilliant blue flowers from summer to early autumn. Erect lancelike green leaves	also grows well in water
Lysichiton americanus Z 7	H 1.2m/4ft	plant in wet soil in half-shade	unpleasantly scented yellow flowers in early spring. Large glaucous green leaves	best where summers are cool
Matteuccia struthiopteris Z 4	H 45–60cm/18–24in	plant in moist well-drained acidic soil in shade or half-shade	lush feathery fronds rising from a central crown in the shape of a shuttlecock	
Nymphaea candida 'Wenzelii'	H 10cm/4in	plant in water in sun or half-shade	small compact star-shaped white flowers with bright yellow stamens in summer. Floating circular dark green leaves	
N. 'Firecrest'	H 15cm/6in	as above	fragrant deep pink flowers with orange-red stamens in summer. Floating circular midgreen leaves	in water plant 15–45cm/6–18in deep
N. 'Marliacea chromatella'	H 15cm/6in	as above	soft glistening cup-shaped yellow flowers in summer. Floating circular dark green leaves mottled and spotted red brown	in water plant 15–60cm/6–24in deep
N. odorata 'Alba'	H 15cm/6in	as above	beautifully scented cup-shaped pure white flowers in summer. Floating circular bright apple-green leaves	in water plant 15–60cm/6–24in deep
N. pygmaea var *alba*	H 5cm/2in	plant in shallow water, up to 15cm/6in deep, in sun	tiny white flowers, 3cm/1in across, with translucent petals and golden centers in summer. Floating circular dark green leaves	slow growing
N.p. 'Helvola'	H 5cm/2in	as above	miniature soft yellow flowers in summer. Floating circular dark green leaves heavily mottled with rich brown	as above
Osmunda regalis Z 3	H 120–150cm/48–60in	plant in wet soil in shade or half-shade	pale green fronds turn russet in autumn	young fronds are edible
Rheum palmatum var *rubrum* Z 4	H 180–250cm/72–96in	plant in moist soil in half-shade	panicles of cream-white, pink or crimson flowers, in summer. Large deeply cut five-lobed red-brown leaves	

— GENERAL INDEX —

—PLANT INDEX—

— PUBLISHERS' ACKNOWLEDGMENTS —

The publishers would like to thank the following for their help in producing this book:
Patricia Shears, Joanna Chisholm, Jonathan Hilton and Susan Conder for additional editorial work, and Susan Berry for initial editorial help and advice.
Claudine Meissner and Anne Fisher for additional design work.
Paul Meyer for horticultural advice.
Nancy Jones for the index.
Susan George for clerical help.

Thanks also to the following for supplying reference material for illustration:
Gary St John Newnes at Artech, Unit 15, Burmarsh Workshops, Marsden Street, London, Bonham Bazeley at Highfield Nurseries, Whiteminster, and the Science Department at Holloway School, London.

EDITOR
Sarah Mitchell

ART EDITORS
Louise Tucker
Caroline Hillier

PICTURE RESEARCHER
Anne Fraser

TYPESETTING
Bookworm Typesetting, Manchester

REPRODUCTION
Universal Colour Scanning Ltd, Hong Kong

ILLUSTRATORS
Artwork   Paul Cox
Garden plans   Robin Williams
Cover border   Michael Craig

GARDEN DESIGNERS
Mrs Barclay 118
Mrs Beaumont 17
Mr & Mrs van Bennekom-Scheffer 105
Mr & Mrs Canneman-Philipse 58–63
John Codrington 32–39
R J Dykes III 28–31
Hillier and Hilton 71
Roger & John Last 51, 96–107
Arabella Lennox-Boyd 64–67
Mr & Mrs Levitan 130–133
Rosemary Verey 85, 89, 90 and front cover
Mr & Mrs Voorwijk 92

PHOTOGRAPHERS
Heather Angel 104, 123
Peter Baistow 84, 91
Michael Boys Syndication 52
Geoff Dann 13, 42, 114, all © FLL
Henk Dijkman 127
Ken Druse 24, 54
Inge Espen-Hansen 108, 112, 129(b)
Derek Fell 11, 74, 86, 111, 128, 130, 131, 132
Robin Fletcher/Natural Image 126(b)
Bob Gibbons/Natural Image 46, 109, 129(t)
Liz Gibbons/Natural Image 93
John Glover 122
Jerry Harpur 34, 51, 71, 85, 100
Marijke Heuff (Amsterdam) 19, 47, 62, 75, 92, 105, 106, 107
Jacqui Hurst 17 © FLL, 43(l), 110, 113(b), 117, 118 © FLL, 120(l & r)
Andrew Lawson 90
Arabella Lennox-Boyd 66
Georges Lévêque 1, 9, 58, 59, 60, 61, 69, 70, 81, front & back cover
Polly Lyster 18
Tania Midgley 64, 65, 121, 126(t)
Carole Ottesen 28, 29, 30
Hugh Palmer 22, 32, 33, 103, 124
Philippe Perdereau 12, 21, 23, 43(r), 50, 115, 116, 125
Clay Perry 2, 37 (Weidenfeld & Nicolson Ltd), 96, 98, 99
Gary Rogers 113(t)
David Russell 82
Ianthe Ruthven 97
Scala/Firenze 10
Elizabeth Whiting & Assoc/Gary Chowanetz 83
George Wright 15